CONTENTS

"I can't believe the level of tennis that I got to see in my career, the shots hit, the records that were broken, and the records that continue to be broken. Thanks to Murray, Novak, Roger and Rafa for playing the game at a higher level than it have ever been played."

Andy Roddick-Former World #1 Tennis Player and 2003 U.S. Open Champion

"To my incredibly beautiful wife, Carmen, I love you with all my heart. Thank you for

*your patience on this project as I dedicate
this book to you. Also, thank you for sharing
the love of the game of tennis with me."*

THE WHY
PURPOSE OF
BOOK

Purpose

The purpose of this book is to capture a fan's perspective of the greatest era in men's professional tennis. I want this book to serve the diehard tennis fans. I also want what makes these four individuals the outstanding tennis players they are, where we can learn and apply to our everyday lives.

This will be a non-fiction book that will combine the love of tennis and self development.

We have Roger Federer, Raphael Nadal, Novak Djokovic, and Andy Murray. Roger and Novak are arguably the two greatest all around tennis players ever. Nadal is the greatest clay court player ever, which is undisputed with to this date ten French Open titles. Andy Murray has hung with the other three and is one of the most important tennis players by being the first Great Britain male to win Wimbledon since 1936. Andy accomplished that feat in 2013.

I will cover many of their epic matches that made many of the fans glued to the television. The ones that come to mind are the 2008 Wimbledon Final between Rafa and Roger as well as the 2012 Australian Open Final between Novak and Rafa. Of course there is Andy's first triumph in the 2012 U.S. Open as well.

I also want to capture the minds and hearts of these four champions. Andy had to overcome the pressure of a Great Britain not winning a Grand Slam major in decades. Andy is also a two time Olympic gold medalist and reached number one in the world in 2016.

Raphael Nadal is arguably the greatest warrior tennis has ever seen. There is no player more mentally tough and determined to win a match. He plays every point like it is his last point. He wears down his opponents both mentally and physically. Clay court tennis is the most difficult and taxing surface to play tennis on, and Rafa has just annihilated the record books. Not only do I want to capture his tenacity, but I also want to capture how Rafa rebounded in 2017 to become the number one player in the world after being written off in 2015 and 2016.

For Novak Djokovic, he could be the most interesting story. Novak grew up during in extremely troublesome times in Serbia. Novak had to survive through two wars growing up. Novak has also had some adversity after winning his first major at age 20. Novak considered quitting the game in 2010. After soul searching and changing up his routine, including his diet, Novak went to dominate 2011 by winning three majors and becoming number one in the world. Novak is arguably the greatest return of server ever. Novak is such an incredible defender who shrinks the court like no other. Not only is he a great defender, Novak is also a great all around player turning defense to offense.

Roger Federer is the first male tennis player to win 20 Grand Slam majors. Roger is considered by many tennis experts as the greatest of all time, which many refer today as the G.O.A.T. To this day, Roger has won 8 Wimbledon titles. He is also the only player to capture at least five majors titles each in three of the four majors. If Novak is the quickest player ever, then Roger is the greatest shot maker ever. Roger plays the game with ease, grace, and beauty. Perhaps Roger owns the greatest forehand in men's tennis history. Because his game is so beautiful, it is easy look past in what truly has made Roger such a great champion. Many do not look at how hard he works both mentally and physically on his game.

Roger has showed grit and heart in some tough matches in his career. His toughness was not really recognized until the 2017 Australian Open. I will cover Roger's knee injury that ended his 2016 season and how he came back to face down his biggest rival Raphael Nadal in 2017, including the epic Australian Open Final.

To be completely transparent, I am not a former professional tennis player nor am I a tennis writer. I am a diehard tennis fan who has followed the game for over 40 years now. I do play tennis at a club level and love the game.

INTRODUCTION

INTRODUCTION

Have you ever wondered how elite athletes rise to the occasion time and again? Sure, it's exciting to watch from the stands or on TV but imagine the immense pressure to perform they are feeling in that moment- all eyes on them, knowing the next series of events can mean the difference between glory and defeat. I've long been fascinated by these hero-type characters and what makes them different from their other extremely talented peers. I've also wondered in what ways their successes might be lessons for each of us to learn from.

Over the years, my passion for sports has developed into a desire to study the elements that make the greatest champions who they are. I may never know what it's like to serve for Championship Point at Wimbledon, but sometimes performing in our own jobs or making a presentation to a new client can feel like a pressure cooker. The skill and mental toughness displayed by our greatest champions can shed some light on how to navigate our own life challenges.

I grew up as a sports fan in New England and there was no shortage of teams in the greater Boston area to follow. Aside from the major American sports like baseball, basketball, football, and hockey I was also an avid fan of boxing, track and field, and occasionally the Olympics. Like many young kids I couldn't get enough of the athletic feats and larger-than-life personas of our best-known sportsmen and women of the era.

My eventual passion for, and life-long love of, tennis was born in the 70's when my father began playing recreationally with his business partners. The growing popularity of the sport meant more television coverage of matches and with it my interest in the game grew. The first players I remember were Bjorn Borg, Chris Evert, Billie Jean King, Jimmy Connors, Martina Navratilova and John McEnroe. During the late 1970's, largely because of these incredible athletes, there was a major tennis boom. More and more tennis courts were being built around the country to accommodate a growing population of tennis enthusiasts.

Watching tennis evolve over the years was incredibly exciting. Both the technology and the physical abilities of the athletes changed the game in so many ways. The move from wood racquets to titanium, and the incorporation of new string technology helped to make the game faster. The athletes themselves needed to adjust to keep up with the innovations. Players were already used to training rigorously all year round, but their regimens now incorporated cutting-edge science to implement fitness, cross-training, and nutrition. Ivan Lendl and Martina Navratilova were amongst the leaders in this new direction of the sport.

In the 1990's tennis was dominated by the superb Pete Sampras- the greatest tennis player that I had ever seen up to that point. His game was fast and powerful and his place in tennis history was long-cemented even before he had won his record 13th grand slam major at Wimbledon in 2000. The trajectory of his career is a mere footnote in this introduction but the phenomenal level to which he played was most certainly a precursor of the players that were yet to come.

Fast forward to the year 2002 and I, along with other tennis spectators, would witness the 'changing of the guard' of sorts for the sport. Pete Sampras came in as the 17th seed after having drastically struggled with his game since that record setting 2000 Wimbledon Championship. I remember this clearly because I decided to attend the U.S. Open that year.

I arrived for the 3rd round day session in the middle weekend of the event. Sampras was scheduled to play the next day against hard-serving lefty Greg Rusedski. I was at the top of Arthur Ashe stadium able to view the entire grounds of the tennis center. In the practice court next to us I saw Sampras practicing with a left-handed player in preparation for his next match. Glancing over at the other courts I spotted the usual suspects like Alex Corretja and Tommy Haas- tour mainstays that had their own fan followings. Nearby an up-and-coming player was beginning to draw the attention of crowds.

Practicing a few courts away from Pete Sampras was Roger Federer.

Of course, I knew who Roger Federer was. I remember him dismantling the U.S. in the 2000 Davis Cup and dethroning Pete at Wimbledon in 2001. Yet, this was the first time I had seen Federer in person. As great as Sampras' game looked, Federer's technical ability was incredible to watch. I kept one eye on Sampras and one on Federer. I always thought Sampras made the game look easy. Yet watching Federer practice, he displayed a grace and fluidity of movement that was on another level. It was breathtaking to watch. I thought to myself that Roger looked like a future number one ranked player in the world if he could put it all together.

Pete Sampras ended up winning the 2002 U.S. Open and, once again, he was anointed the greatest men's tennis player by many experts and writers. He ended up retiring on top with 14 major Championships. As a Sampras fan I was impressed and happy with his performance. Yet, I never forgot what I saw in that practice session with Federer.

It took less than a year for Roger Federer to win his first major championship when he won Wimbledon in 2003. Of course, he became the number one player in the world, many times over, and took the game to the next level by surpassing Sampras' record number of majors by winning his 15th title in 2009 in a near-perfect, marathon Wimbledon final against Andy Roddick.

Remembering back to when I had first seen his game in-person on the practice courts at Flushing Meadows, even I could never have imagined what Federer would do to take men's tennis to another level. Even more so, it is unfathomable that at the age of 36 (which he will be at the end of 2018) he is still in contention for every major title and took home the Australian Open at the beginning of this year. He is not just thriving but continuing to dominate. Roger Federer's has been incredibly consistent for the past 15 years since Wimbledon in 2003.

While it's easy to focus on Roger Federer, he isn't alone in taking the men's game to a new level. Just as Federer was taking the number one ranking, a player from Mallorca, Spain was on the rise. Rafael Nadal was a product of a major tennis boom happening in Spain. Alex Corretja, Juan Carlos Ferrero, Carlos Moya, Alberto Costa, and recently retired Sergi Brugeuera had already been carrying the torch for Spain- including Davis Cup wins in 2000 and 2004. The successes of these players came especially from clay, but many of them could play on all surfaces. This prolific talent paved the way for Nadal to step onto the stage.

Known as 'Rafa' to the tennis world, Rafael Nadal's game is all-out, intense, and full of passion. He plays every point like it is his last. Nadal's legend, like Federer's, grows with the number of majors he wins- 16 majors to date as I write this. No small feat to surpass Sampras' record and completely dominate on clay with 10 of those majors coming on the tricky surface. A career Grand Slam and holding the number one ranking for four years is proof enough of his place in tennis history. Nadal is one of the most tenacious players ever to step foot on the court.

Also known for his passion is another seminal figure in this era of men's tennis- Novak Djokovic. The Serbian-born player overcame an upbringing in a war-torn country, in which waiting in long lines for basic needs such as bread was the norm. Through his skillful baseline coverage and incredible all-around game, he climbed to the top of the world rankings. Known as a defensive player, Djokovic is also a great offensive player. Possibly no other player in the game can transition from defense to offense so quickly. His return of serve is amongst the greatest ever seen and is especially difficult to win points against because he covers the court beautifully. With 12 majors thus far, including 6 Australian Open titles, Djokovic has overcome all the adversities in his life to become a champion.

At about the same time that Djokovic was making his move among the tennis elite, a man from Scotland named Andy Murray began to rise in prominence as well. Coming from the United Kingdom is a special distinction for a tennis player because once a he begins to display a certain level of talent, the whisperings of whether he will or can win Wimbledon is a huge burden to bear. Great Britain had been waiting for one of their own to win Wimbledon since Fred Perry in 1936. Englishman Tim Henman largely played that hopeful role for over a decade. And while he was a talented and well-loved player in his own right, he came up short of winning Wimbledon for his home nation. Although he hasn't amassed the same number of major wins as the other champions highlighted, he persevered and became a great tennis champion himself. In 2016 Murray dethroned Djokovic's reign as number one player in the world but more significantly he ended the Wimbledon drought by winning the title in 2013.

As a lifelong tennis fan, I've found that observing how these elite athletes navigate the ups and downs of their sporting careers is inspiring. I wanted to capture some of the lessons that I've learned from them and pay homage to some of the most exhilarating moments in sports history.

In this book, we will focus on the mindset of these four champions (Federer, Nadal, Djokovic, and Murray) who created what I believe to be the greatest era in men's tennis. Naturally, all of them had great talent and an incredible work ethic. Yet all of them had unique character traits that made them champions which we can learn from and apply to all areas of our lives- our emotional life, health, relationships, finances, business, etc.

We can have our own successes and victories like the Big Four do on the tennis court. We will look at how we can apply Roger's consistency year after year being a top player. We'll look at Nadal's tenacity and how he plays with intensity and passion. Djokovic is an example of overcoming adversity in his childhood, but also a lesson in overcoming the shadow of Federer and Nadal. Lastly, we will look at how perseverance can bring us success as in the example of Andy Murray who, after getting knocked down quite a few times, finally reached the top.

PERSEVERANCE
ANDY MURRAY

PERSEVERENCE

"There is a relentlessness that goes with being me. I have a sense of what I do is never good enough. Perhaps that is what keeps me playing."

- From Andy Murray's autobiography 'Seventy-Seven'

Perseverance is what has made Andy Murray's professional tennis career. Among is his many great accomplishments (those of which are still likely to come) was his win at Wimbledon in 2013. That win will be remembered in history because it ended the 77-year drought for the Brits. But this feat is just as remarkable because of is Murray's journey to overcome the immense pressure that plagued his early tennis career and his unique ability to break through that singular challenge that had stifled so many great British players before him. Yes, Andy Murray's immense talent has been the main ingredient in his success, but his grit and perseverance have pushed him above the pack to the highest echelons of men's tennis.

Early Life:

Born May 15, 1987, Andy Murray grew up in a tennis family. His mother was a former professional player and has continued her engagement with the sport as a coach for the Scottish national team. Andy's brother, Jamie Murray, is a top men's doubles player and has won five majors. His pedigree in the sport was well established from the beginning.

While he had a relatively normal upbringing, his childhood was touched by tragedy. At the age of 8 years old he was attending Dunblane Primary School when it suffered (what was at the time) the worst mass school shooting in history. A gunman had entered a classroom full of children, aged between 5 and 6, and opened fire. Sixteen students and one teacher were killed. Murray was at the school that day and although he was not in that classroom, the effects of that event stayed with him even as an adult. In fact, he returned to Dunblane Primary School to celebrate his Wimbledon titles and the Olympic Gold Medal as a way to encourage students and shed a positive light on the school.

Promising Young Career:

At the age of 15, Andy Murray's exceptional talent was already recognizable. The expectations of what he could go on to accomplish in his professional tennis career were high and precipitated a move to Spain to develop his talent. This relocation was in part because of the weather in Scotland (not conducive to year-round training) and also at the encouragement of his friend Rafael Nadal who was also on the fast-track to professional tennis success and enjoying the benefits of a full training schedule in his home country. During these years in the late 1990's while training in Spain, Murray learned discipline, hard work, and what it took to play at the highest levels of competition.

Setbacks and Disappointments:

After such a promising junior tennis career, his transition into the professional tennis circuit was not as smooth. Several of his contemporaries that came through at the same time were already gaining superstar status and fulfilling the prophesies that were made about him. The expectation that he should transition from Championship tennis at the Junior level to Grand Slam contender early in the first few years of joining the ATP did not materialize for Murray. The confidence of being a stand-out in his early years started to give way to feelings of doubt. A turning point came at the 2010 Australian Open, when he started to feel that he might not win a major if he kept on the same track. Despite this discouragement, he loved the game and decided to keep working.

The next year in 2011, he reached the Australian Open finals only to lose the Championship to Novak Djokovic. Despite the disappointment, he regrouped and had a solid clay court season culminating in a semi-finals appearance in the French Open. It seemed that Andy Murray was finally getting closer to the goal of a grand slam win- he was becoming a top contender at each tournament.

A New Approach:

With the momentum of the 2011 season and his appearance in the later rounds of the Grand Slams, Andy Murray decided to hire Ivan Lendl to mentor him. Lendl, the one of the greatest tennis champions, also known for his work ethic, shared some experiences in his career that Murray could relate to. Like Murray, Lendl had initially lost multiple grand slam finals before breaking through and having a hall-of-fame career. Lendl eventually won 8 majors and was ranked world number 1 for 270 weeks. Murray knew Lendl would be able to infuse a new approach that could help him reach the next level.

One problem that Murray had been grappling with was overcoming and working through his own self-doubt. In his autobiography, Murray talks about the pressure and emotions that come along with being an athlete in the public eye.[1] Andy felt the pressure not only to win for himself but he also felt the weight of Britain on his shoulders.

The Breakthrough:

In 2012, with Ivan Lendl in his coaching box, Murray produced some of the best tennis of his career. The start of the season would see Murray building on the strong from he had developed the previous year. There was another Murray-Djokovic rematch in the Australian Open, but this time in the semi-finals. Again, Djokovic bested Murray in this matchup, but the five-setter was far more competitive than their previous meeting at the Australian Open and could have gone either way. At the French Open Murray reached the quarter-finals and lost against Spaniard, and clay-specialist, David Ferrer. These strong showings would set up quite the summer for Murray.

Next up was Wimbledon. From the outset, the tournament was going to be a challenge- Murray had been given a difficult draw. He rose to the occasion and managed to get past premier players such as Nikolai Davydenko, Ivo Karlovic, Marcos Baghdatis, and Marin Cilic. In the quarterfinals awaited David Ferrer again- the opponent who had just ousted him from Roland Garros a few months ago. This time Murray exacted his revenge for the French Open loss by defeating Ferrer in four grueling sets. Awaiting in the semis was Frenchman Jo-Wilred Tsonga, whom Murray dismissed in 4 sets.

With the win against Tsonga, Andy Murray earned a spot in his first Wimbledon final and an opportunity to be the first British player to win the title. He was in prime position to fulfill the ultimate dream. But one thing was in his way- Roger Federer. This was Murray's fourth major final appearance but despite the excellent tournament that Murray was having, Roger Federer was the favorite in the final.

Federer, already a six-time Wimbledon champion had just beat Novak Djokovic on his journey to the final. He had big crowd support and has always been a favorite at the tournament. Despite this, Murray was able to get off to a fast start winning his first set in a major final. Unfortunately for Murray, the rains came and the roof of Centre Court was closed. As a result, the match became an indoor affair and created conditions that heavily favored Federer's style of play. Federer would be in the zone for the next three sets, allowing him to conquer his seventh Wimbledon Championship.

It was not meant to be that year for Murray and he was devastated to have come so close only to lose in the final. During the post-match on-court interviews, Murray gave an incredibly emotional speech thanking everyone for all of their support and acknowledging that he was getting closer. Rather than fixate on what could have been, Murray was proud of the growth of his game and the accomplishment of making it so deep into the tournament.[2]

Coincidentally, the Summer Olympics were also in London and Andy Murray would have another chance to play on the grounds at Wimbledon. It was evident that the tournament loss to Roger Federer did not break Murray. Murray would go on to defeat rival Novak Djokovic in the semis and set up another tournament finals showdown with Federer. This time Murray got the best of Federer and pulled out the win in 3 straight sets, capturing the Olympic Gold Medal in his home country.

Fresh off his Olympic victory, Andy Murray was ready to take on the U.S. Open- the last major of the tennis season. He underperformed during the summer hardcourt tournaments at Toronto and Cincinnati due to exhaustion after the Olympics, still Murray looked ready to make a serious run at the U.S. Open. Murray advanced to the semifinals where he would defeat Tomas Berdych of the Czech Republic and this set up a finals showdown with Djokovic.

Early on, Murray jumped ahead with a two-set lead. But ever the competitor, Djokovic came back to tie up the game and force a fifth set. It appeared that Djokovic had all the momentum going into the fifth set. Prior to the fifth set, Murray took a break to the men's room and composed himself. Showing zero signs of fatigue, Murray kept his resolve and went on to taking the fifth set and winning the U.S. Open Championship. With this win he brought home Britain's first men's major title since Fred Perry in 1936.

HOW ANDY
PERSEVERED

Rising Star and Disappointments

A long with Novak, Rafa, and others in his generation, Andy was considered someone who was going to be number one in the world and win majors. The summer of 2008 was Andy's coming out party as a future great in the game. He had beaten Roger earlier in the year and defeated Novak twice in that summer. At the U.S. Open he defeated Rafa who was coming off a French and Wimbledon. Rafa also won the Olympic Gold Medal and displaced Roger as the number one player in the world. Even though Andy lost to Roger in the finals, the future was looking incredibly bright.

Fans and media believed that Andy would win majors. What we did not know is that Andy's first major title would not come until four years later in 2012 U.S. Open after making his first major finals appearance.

Fans and media even thought that Andy was among the favorites heading into the Australian Open in 2009. Andy would lose in the quarterfinals. Andy would win some big tournaments in 2009 and get a firm hold on the number four ranking. However, Andy did not win a major in 2009.

Many thought Andy's time would come again in the 2010 Australian Open. He played extremely well and worked tremendously hard improving his offensive game in the offseason. Andy would make his second major finals. However, he ran into a red hot Roger Federer. Even though Andy fought back in the third set after being two sets down, Roger would win in three sets and earn his 16th major title. The remainder of 2010 was solid, and even reached the # 3 ranking before falling back to # 4 at the end of the year.

Once again, Andy would come back in 2011 determined to breakthrough in the majors. He earned another trip to the Australian Open Finals, but lost again in three sets to Novak Djokovic. In three major finals, Andy had yet to win a set. Andy would continue to play well in 2011 by winning some big tournaments. Yet, he came up once again empty handed in the majors.

Jumping Over the Biggest Hurdle:

2012 started the same way the three previous years for Andy. Andy played well in the Australian Open and lost a hard fought semifinals to the eventual champion, Novak Djokovic. Andy would continue to see his peers win majors. However, Andy continued to work diligently and waited for his opportunity. Being from Britain, the fans and the media were waiting for their first men's champion in Britain since 1936. What would better to capture his first major than Wimbledon? Wimbledon was the longest traditional tournament, and it was Andy's home major.

Andy would have other major finals appearance. However, he now had earned a trip to the finals at Wimbledon. With nearly everyone in Great Britain behind him, Andy set his sights on a Wimbledon title. Despite finally winning his first set in a final, Andy would fall to legend Roger Federer in four sets. The unfortunate occurrence for Andy was the rain and the roof was closed for the last three sets of the match. Roger was still considered the greatest indoor tennis player at the time. As a result his level rose, and he would win his 7th Wimbledon title.

With the 2012 Summer Olympics in London, Wimbledon was the site for tennis event. Andy would extract his revenge on Roger at the same place a month earlier and capture his first Olympic Gold Medal over Roger in three sets.

Approximately a month later, Andy found himself once again in a major final at the 2012 U.S. Open. It was exactly four years later after his first major finals appearance. It was fifth over-all appearance in a major final. His opponent would be Novak. Andy would get off to the start he wanted by taking the first two sets. Novak, however; stormed back by taking the next two sets. Going to a fifth and decisive set, Novak had the momen-tum. Andy took a bathroom break before the fifth set. When he looked in the mirror, he told himself that he was going to win this match.

Andy would come out on fire taking the match from Novak and won the set 6-2 to capture his first major title. The 2012 U.S. Open Men's Singles Champion was Andy Murray. Everything Andy worked for had finally paid off.

Wimbledon Champion:

Even though Andy broke through in 2012, nothing was more significant to Great Britain and Andy Murray than a Wimbledon title. He almost did it in 2012. In 2013, he was determined to get it done. Andy missed the French Open in order to squarely focus on winning Wimbledon. Andy would get to the finals after some hard fought matches throughout the fortnight, in-cluding battling back from two sets down in the quarterfinals to defeat Spain's Fernando Verdasco in five sets.

2011 Wimbledon Champion, Novak Djokovic would be Andy's opponent. This time, Andy would become the hero of Great Britain by defeating Novak in three sets to win Wimbledon. Andy won his second major title and became the first British male to win Wimbledon in 77 years. The pressure was tremendous. Yet, Andy was still able to deliver. It was such a tremendous clutch performance and Andy could always say that he is a Wimbledon Champion.

Injuries and the Comeback:

The beginning of 2014 would be Andy's biggest test when it comes to perseverance and determination. Late in 2013, Andy would have to undergo back surgery. Thus, 2014 was going to likely be a bridge year. Andy would have to comeback slowly and work his way back into condition to be a top player. With back injuries, it is difficult to know if he could make it all the way back to an elite level.

2014 would be a trying season with early round losses and upsets. It was also going to be a challenge mentally as well as physically if he could make it all the way back. Despite the obstacles, Andy would not relent. Andy would continue to get stronger throughout the year and even qualified for the ATP Finals at the end of the year.

2015 would be another step forward from 2014 as Andy continued to regain his confidence. Andy would earn a trip to the finals in the 2015 Australian Open and lose to Djokovic. Andy also got the semifinals in the French Open and Wimbledon. Andy would have his first win over rival Novak Djokovic in the summer in Montreal. Also, Andy achieved his highest ranking ever by finishing number two for the year.

Number One:

In 2016, Andy was riding the momentum of finishing #2 for the first time ever. However, Andy would have to overcome his biggest challenge ever. That challenge was to dethrone Novak Djokovic to become the number one player in the world. Novak was coming off perhaps the greatest season ever in 2015 a men's tennis player has ever had. Novak would continue that momentum by defeating Andy in the 2016 Australian Open finals. After earning his first French Open Final, Andy would lose to Novak again. Novak, at this point, seemed to have a firm grasp of finishing 2016 as the number one player.

Andy would fight back by capturing his 2nd Wimbledon title and then winning the Olympic Gold Medal late in the summer. It would also be his 2nd Gold Medal in Men's singles.

Despite falling in the quarterfinals in the U.S. Open, Andy still had the momentum and a chance to finish the year at number one. What Andy did then was remarkable. Andy would win his next three tournaments and earned the number one ranking for the first time ever. However, he would have to play great in the ATP Finals to hold on and finish the year at number one. Andy was able to win every match heading to the finals. However, Novak also went undefeated and would earn a trip to the finals as well. Thus whoever won would not only win the tournament, they would finish the year at number one. Andy would not let Novak in the match and was able to win in two sets. As a result, Andy would finish 2016 as the number one player in the world for the first time ever and etched his name in the history books. Andy Murray became a tennis legend.

Becoming a Great Clay Court Player:

Being born and raised in Scotland, the one surface that Andy did not get to play frequently on was clay. Despite being a great return of serve player, counterpuncher, and outstanding mover, Andy was never comfortable playing on the clay surface.

Andy would be one of the favorites and every tournament throughout his career. However, that was not the case on the clay surface. Andy would go deep into many majors and other big tournaments. On clay, it was early exits.

However, Andy was determined to become a great clay court player as well. Slowly but surely, he continued to play on clay more often and worked diligently on his movement on clay and got used to the bounce of the ball on the surface. Andy would start finding himself go from a second round exit to earning a trip to the quarterfinals. Finally, Andy was able to see himself in the semifinals at the French Open.

Patience and persistence paid off in 2015 and 2016, where Andy defeated the King of Clay, Rafael Nadal, in Madrid to capture his first big clay title. He then defeated a red hot Novak Djokovic in 2016 at Rome to capture another big title in Rome. Despite losing to Novak in the 2016 French Open, Andy would earn his first major finals appearance at the French Open. Thus, Andy had earned a trip to the finals in all four majors.

WHAT WE CAN LEARN FROM ANDY MURRAY

I am always reminded of a quote from Anthony Robbins where he says, "When it seems impossible, when it seems like nothing is going to work, you're only a few millimeters away from making it happen". I truly believe that Andy has applied this quote throughout his professional tennis career.

In chapter 5 on page 109 in Andy's autobiography "Seventy Seven", Andy says "there is a relentlessness that goes with being me. I have a sense of what I do is never good enough. Perhaps that is what keeps me playing".

Perseverance, I believe is what has made Andy Murray's career. Perseverance, I believe is more important than talent. Yes, Andy is talented. However, Andy's time came in an era where other players are perhaps even more talented than him. Thus, Andy truly needed have the grit and perseverance in order to accomplish two Wimbledon championships and the number one ranking. So what can we learn from Andy Murray? How can we apply perseverance in our everyday lives?

Trust The Process:

I believe the first attribute we need is to trust, love, and embrace the process. In many ways, Andy exemplifies what success is all about. Success is defined in many different ways. Looking from the outside sometimes we do not realize what an Andy Murray, a LeBron James, or a Lionel Messi goes through in order to get to the level where they are at.

We have a tendency to look from the outside and say these great superstars or an actor or celebrities have such a charmed life. Yet, we are not aware of all the sacrifices that were made along the way for even the minimal success that was achieved.

As we can see from this graph, Andy's journey is definitely more on the right. It shows that we are going to experience many ups and downs along the way on the journey. We too are going to experience many of these obstacles along the way in our relationships, business, finances (especially if we are in the stock market), health, and even our emotions.

Sometimes we don't get that promotion just like Andy will lose to Federer or Djokovic. Sometimes, we don't get the news we want from the doctor's offices or we go through a down cycle with our spouse or significant other. We need to be strong like Andy, get up the next day, hit the practice court, look on what we can improve upon, and continue to get better.

This is why loving what we do is so incredibly important. If Andy did not love the game of tennis as much as he does, perhaps he would not be able to sustain the high level of tennis he has given us over the years. We have to love what we do in business or find something that we love what we do. Andy's love for the game enabled him to enjoy the journey along the way in order to get to his destination.

We too have to understand that the journey is the reward and the key to happiness. It is not the destination. We at times do not have control over the results. Andy has no control on how Nadal and Djokovic prepare or do on the court. Andy does have control on how he prepares and does on the court. It is the same for us. We have no control over our boss and co workers. We have no control on what our significant other, friend, or family member is going to say or do. We do have control on what we say, do, and how we are going to act in situations.

Lastly, we also enjoy the process by developing a why and always reminding ourselves our why. Why is important for us to get up every morning go to work, start our business, take that class at night, or get that degree or certificate? Andy had his why every time he stepped out on the tennis court to practice and continue to improve his game.

The Past Does Not Equal The Future:

The second way to develop perseverance and what Andy used is to always realize that the past does not equal the present and the future. I think it is extremely important to learn, grow, and appreciate our past. It is also important to use the past as a reference that we can succeed just like Andy winning the junior US Open or when he won a major tournament or when he did beat his rival.

It is important though not to live in the past and dwell on it either. We can enter into a new relationship always comparing our past relationships. We also cannot anticipate that a new relationship is going to be the same as a previous relationship. Andy was very careful to not go into a match against an opponent looking back at their previous match.

A great example of not dwelling on the previous match is when Andy met Roger Federer in the final of the 2012 Olympics to decide the Gold Medal. Andy said it perfectly in "Seventy Seven" chapter 3 page 79, "the final would be a rematch against Roger for the Olympic Gold. It was being billed as a revenge mission, but going into matches trying to revenge for something that happened in the past usually doesn't help at all. I always focus on the task in hand and not dwell on what I should or might have done before. There is nothing you can do to bring it back."

As we can see Andy never looks at the past matches. He goes into a match with a clean slate. Yes, he will apply some new tactics and strategies that he did not do in the previous match. Psychologically though, he is not focused on his previous matches with his current opponent.

Andy was also able to leverage that Roger was in a unique situation. Roger had never played for the gold medal in men's singles. Thus, he was on the same experience level as Roger. Andy did not let up at all and played a near flawless tennis match to beat Roger and win the gold.

We need to apply the same principles here if we were in a sales meeting. We cannot look at previous meetings where we did not land the account. We need make the necessary adjustments, learn from the past, and appreciate what we do well. With a mindset like Andy, we will be able to become successful in any area of business.

Be Flexible When Needed:

The third and final thing that we can learn from Andy is to change our approach if something is not consistently working. Yes, we work hard; we practice hard in order to improve. However, we need to anticipate changes and get the necessary help we need to put us at the top.

Andy did this twice in his career and it was the same action. That action was to hire Ivan Lendl as his coach. The best ways we can achieve what we desire is to get a role model. Get a role model who was once where you are (or were) and is now at the level you want to get to.

Ivan Lendl's hiring made perfect sense to Andy because like Andy, Ivan lost many finals of a major before winning his first one. Ivan's first major final was at the 1980 French Open and did not finally win his first major final until four years later at the 1984 French Open. He finally won it on his 4th attempt. Once

Lendl won his first, we went on to win seven more majors and was number one in the world for three consecutive years. Thus, he would be the perfect role model for Andy.

As a result of hiring Ivan, Andy went on to win the Gold Medal and his first two major titles in one year.

The second time Andy looked to Ivan was to unseat Novak as the number one player in the world. Novak was dominating the men's game at the time. Andy knew he needed an answer to catch and overtake Novak and that was to hire Ivan again. This 2nd hiring resulted in Andy's 2nd Wimbledon title and a 25 match winning streak which enabled Andy to become number one in the world for 2016.

Just like Andy, we can hire or find role models for ourselves. My mentor's brother actually hired a gentleman who became a multi millionaire in Canada from real estate. My mentor's brother desired the same outcome as the millionaire and met him while he was in construction. My mentor's brother had the courage to approach the millionaire to teach him the real estate business. As a result, my mentor's brother is now a multi millionaire with a beautiful lake house in British Columbia and other real estate property in the greater Vancouver area.

We can also look for mentors through biographies, books, and even the internet which is completely driven by content.

Thus hiring a mentor is a great tool to change our approach to get our desired results. It is can be useful to have a mentor in our relationships, health, spirituality, and even time management.

I believe Andy's perseverance on and off the tennis court provides such an outstanding example for all of us, both children and adult.

2013 WIMBLEDON FINAL

To understand the pressure on Andy Murray before the 2013 Wimbledon final requires a knowledge of tennis history. Wimbledon is the oldest event in tennis. It is also considered by many the most important tournament, with past champions stating that Wimbledon is the ultimate prize.

Going into 2013, it had been 77 years since a British player had won the men's singles title- the last was Fred Perry in 1936. Tim Henman gave Britain hope in the 90's and early into the 2000's, however he came up against talent from the likes of Pete Sampras, Roger Federer, and Lleyton Hewitt who were dominant on the grass surface. So, when Andy Murray earned a place in the 2012 Wimbledon final, the whole of Great Britain was behind him. However, he fell short that day to Roger Federer and it felt as though a huge opportunity had slipped through his fingers. Murray knew he was only going to get so many opportunities to attempt to win the championship and lift the Wimbledon trophy.

In a remarkable showing, Murray once again was able to reach the final the following year after his first appearance. The 2013 Wimbledon final was a matchup between Andy Murray and Novak Djokovic. Djokovic himself was the winner of the tournament in 2011. The two had encountered each other many times in the recent past at different events. Murray enjoyed a boost of confidence at having recently defeated Djokovic in another big match, the 2012 U.S. Open final. However, with the looming presence of an historic victory, many questioned whether Murray would succumb to nerves throughout the match and at crucial moments. Both men were well matched in respect to their grass court games and had been in fierce competition throughout the last couple of years, so the anticipation for this match was immense.

Set 1:

The match started out great for Murray. He was aggressive from the beginning, getting three break points in the first game. There was also a 20-shot rally to open the match. Murray broke Djokovic's serve in the third game to make it 2-1. Unfortunately, Djokovic broke back immediately to even up the match at 2 games all. Murray would eventually break Djokovic one more time to go up 4-3 and hold on to win the first set 6-4. Both players were relentless. Murray was taking the match right to Djokovic and showing incredible defense, hustle, and poise. Djokovic was playing well, but Murray was the much more the aggressive player in the first set.

Set 2:

The second set was a test of perseverance once again for Murray as Djokovic began to play more aggressively. Breaking Murray early, Djokovic held a 4-1 lead. Instead of allowing Djokovic to claim the second set, Murray showed tremendous grit and fought to extend the second set. His efforts allowed him to break Djokovic to tie the second set 4-4. At 5-5, Murray won the crucial break for the second set at 6-5. Murray would close out the next game with an ace to take two sets to love lead.

Although winning the first two sets is an enormous head start to a match, everyone, especially Murray could see that Djokovic was not going to go away easily. Djokovic has been known for ferocious comebacks, so Murray would have to continue to attack and hold onto the momentum.

Set 3:

The third set started well for Murray who broke Djokovic in the first game. Murray would consolidate the break to go up 2 games to love in the third. However, Djokovic changed things up and started to show a soft touch and drop shot not only to get back into the match, but he also broke Murray consecutively to go up 4 games to 2 in the third set.

Once again, Murray was resilient and fought to prevent the match going into the fourth set. Murray would go on to break Djokovic to get back on serve. At 4-4 in the third set, Murray once again seized the momentum from Djokovic. Murray broke him to serve for the Championship and serve for history. Even staring down the other end of Championship point being served, Novak Djokovic's championship credentials meant he was a competitor you could be expected to battle to the end. Nothing was sewn up or even close to it.

Andy Murray would start the game with an unforced error by Djokovic who hit a shot that sailed long.

15-0 Murray

Murray began to show his nerve though- missing his first serve on two consecutive points. However, Murray went up 30-love on a winner by chasing down a skillful drop shot by Djokovic. Murray would finally hit a clean first serve that Djokovic hit long,

40-0 Murray

With a 40-0 deficit, Djokovic would show tremendous fight and poise climbing all the way back to get it to deuce. Murray and the noisy fans got nervous and quiet. Djokovic was beginning to demonstrate the brilliance he was known for: his tremendous speed and expert shot-making. At deuce, Djokovic got a break point and the opportunity to tie and make the set score 5 games apiece.

However, Murray was relentless. Murray saved the first break point by delivering a huge first serve which gave him deuce #2. With deuce #2 reflected on the scoreboard, Djokovic delivered a beautiful drop shot that just clipped over the net to earn his second breakpoint. Murray had an answer for Djokovic each time and while receiving a second-serve returned a nice winner to make it deuce #3. Once again Djokovic earned a breakpoint by defending against a Murray drop shot and replying with a winner. This gave Djokovic a third breakpoint opportunity.

During the next point, Murray answered with a volley winner and it was back to deuce #4. On a second-serve opportunity, Murray and Djokovic rallied for another great exchange until Djokovic hit a shot into the net.

Murray prepared at the baseline to serve for his fourth opportunity at Championship Point.

At this point, with all of the intensity from this single game alone, the atmosphere in the stadium was electric. Fans were chanting "Andy" over and over again in anticipation of this big moment.

Murray's first serve was in and Djokovic returned with a ball that clipped the line. Murray then hit a strong forehand to Djokovic's backhand. Djokovic hit it into the net. With that unreturned shot, Andy Murray became the 2013 Wimbledon Men's Singles Champion and finally brought home the trophy to Great Britain.

On the scoreboard, the match looked one-sided for Murray. However, the quality of the match did not reflect the score. Djokovic tested Murray to his limits and this is another reason that this win is so outstanding for Murray. Djokovic came close to taking control of the match at several different points, but

Jamie Sierra

Murray would not be denied. It took a tremendous opponent to get the best out of Murray and quite possibly force him to play the match of his life. As a result, Murray has his place in tennis history.

ADVERSITY
NOVAK DJOKOVIC

ADVERSITY

"I know that success does not come at once, it is not a thing achieved overnight. It is the result of many, many, many years of working and trying to achieve goals"

"We only have one life and one body to take care of, and we better do it right. You never know what tomorrow may bring and so we better live this life the best we can and be grateful for everything we have"

-       Novak Djokovic

When I think of Novak Djokovic, I do not just think about one of the greatest players to pick up a tennis racquet. I think of all the adversity he has to overcome on and off the court. He had to overcome adversity as a child going through a war in his country. Novak has also had adversity throughout his career with his health and knowing that he was born at the same time with two other great tennis legends in Federer and Nadal.

At 6'2" and 176 pounds, Novak is the perfect physique for tennis. Novak's game is based on speed, defense, and the return of serve. Novak's speed and defense shrinks the court incredibly making it extremely difficult for his opponents to get winners. It is sort of like threading the needle on the first try.

John McEnroe describes Novak as "the great return of serve"

ever. Novak has an amazing two handed backhand and incredible flexibility to get to balls that is virtually impossible.

Even though Novak relies on his return and defense, he also has an outstanding offensive game with one of the best two handed backhands, followed with a solid serve and forehand. Thus, Novak has an all court game with the likes of Federer. Along with Federer and Nadal, I have never seen any player who can turn defense into offense.

Even thought the purpose of this book is not to depict the GOAT (greatest of all time) in men's tennis, Novak's name has to be mentioned as one of the greatest who ever played the game.

Novak Djokovic's tennis career is a wonderful example of how adversity can shape our successes. From an early age, Djokovic experienced the dangerous uncertainty of living in war-torn Serbia- a situation unfathomable to most of us. And yet through this hardship and some might argue because of it, he was able to emerge as a breakout tennis talent. But even after he escaped from the turmoil of his homeland and was securely on track to join the best men's tennis players on the ATP, he has had to battle with the ups and downs that come along with competing at the highest levels.

Often thought of as obstacles or misfortunate occurrences, the adversities that we face provide challenging moments that we can learn from and overcome. Adversity can be very painful. Yet what is great about this pain is that it affords us the unique opportunity to change for the better- depending on how we use this chance. Novak Djokovic, throughout his life and career, is clearly someone who has learned to harness the power of adversity for good. Adversity has fueled him to become one of the greatest male tennis players of all time.

EARLY YEARS:

Born May 22, 1987 in Belgrade, Serbia, Novak Djokovic is the youngest of the Big Four. He is only 7 days younger than Andy Murray. Djokovic came from an athletic family. His father was a professional skier and happened to be a great soccer player. So, it wasn't a surprise that Novak started in sports early- taking up tennis at the tender age of 4. When he was growing up, the Djokovic family owned both a fast food restaurant and a sports facility. This sports facility included a tennis club, so Djokovic had unlimited access to the courts.

At the age of 6, Djokovic's raw talent was spotted by veteran coach, Jelena Gencic. Gencic was the former coach of tennis superstar Monica Seles. Gencic saw that Djokovic, even at this early age, possessed incredible talent. She had even said at the time she though this young man was the greatest talent she had witnessed since Monica Seles. Gencic was committed to developing the talent that she saw in young Novak. She would spend the next several years coaching Djokovic, but more than that, she became a mentor to him off the court. Gencic introduced him to classical music, insisted he appreciate reading, and encouraged him to write poetry. During this time, he also learned to speak English, German, and Italian. She was able to enrich Novak Djokovic's early childhood in numerous ways that went far beyond the tennis court. Gencic's mentorship was a fortunate happenstance for him.

Meanwhile, the circumstances surrounding his childhood and home country were less kind and generous. Novak Djokovic grew up in Belgrade, Serbia and witnessed the dangers of two wars. As Djokovic describes in his book, *Serve to Win*, 'it was as though we were living in a snow globe and someone had hurled it on the floor." The chaos and upheaval the wars caused in his young life had been incredibly impactful and haunting. Also, in his book, he discusses seeing rockets in the air and the sandy, dusty metallic smell that accompanies these attacks. Even at night, there was no relief. Attacks would happen during the evening, in low visibility, and sirens were going off constantly.

One time, he recounted the sound of a nearby explosion badly startled his mother and caused her to slip and hit her head against the radiator. Living in their regular family home was no longer an option given the proximity of the fighting. Fortunately, Djokovic's aunt owned a property with a bomb shelter. His aunt lived nearby and luckily the whole family was able to huddle together in this shelter and keep safe. This was becoming more of a frequent occurrence as and at one time the Djokovic family stayed in the shelter for 78 consecutive days.

The immediate fear for his and his family's safety was already more than most young people endure, but the economic climate in Serbia caused other hardships on top of this. His parents attempted to make life as normal as possible for the family despite the hours-long wait in lines for simple supplies such as bread. They did this keeping life as normal as possible- meals were served, even if much scanter than before, and they made the choice to prioritize the children's regular interests. Novak would still pursue tennis and continue to play in amateur tournaments. His parents weren't going to get the temporary circumstances have a negative impact on his long-terms goals and aspirations.

This was a birth of fire experience for Novak Djokovic to experience at such a young age. Fortunately, he has since shown, through his own example, that it is possible to turn such adversities into empowering motivators that would give him the tools to succeed in the future.

The dangerous reality of living through a war was something he and his family were unable to escape. But once he accepted that these were the circumstances he was dealt; a certain sense of freedom took over. The situation was out of his hands and he could only control his own behaviors, emotions and the perspective with which he would view life.

Undoubtedly, the early crises in his life helped Djokovic appreciate that the most important things in life are love and appreciating what you have. His values are grounded on these principles because he knows what things can change in an instant. When he catches himself taking something for granted, he always remembers what he has gone through in his past. His early childhood lessons with Gencic both on and off the court, as well as the effects of war created an unlikely sense of open-mindedness and optimism. This mindset paid major dividends when Dr. Igor Cetojevic approached Djokovic in 2010.

NOVAK OVERCOMING ADVERSITY ON THE COURT

Rising In The Rankings, But
Could Not Finish Matches

After winning his first ATP Title in 2006, Novak really broke through in 2007. Novak would beat Roger and Rafa for the first time in his careers. He would also win big titles in Miami and Montreal and rise to the # 3 in the world.

Yet, the only concern was that Novak retired in two matches, including the Wimbledon semifinals against Rafa. Novak also appeared to hit a wall when he lost his last 4 matches of 2007, which was a first round loss in Paris and losing all three of his round robin matches in the ATP Finals.

The feeling at the beginning of 2008 was that Novak was going to continue to progress and get to the next level. The start of 2008 showed every sight that was the case. Novak won his first major at the Australian Open. Novak defeated the two time defending champion Roger Federer in the semifinals in three sets. It would be Roger's first non-clay major loss in three years.

Novak would go on to meet Jo Wilfred Tsonga in the finals and capture his first major title by defeating Tsonga in four sets. Novak had his first major under his belt and would appear to have many more coming.

As 2008 progressed, Novak did post some excellent results. However, he was also feeling the pressure of being one of the top guys. He remained number three.

Yet, Novak would also continue to have trouble finishing matches due to his physical condition. It started in the fourth round against Spain's Tommy Robredo. It was a five set battle, which Novak prevailed. Novak would take two medical time-outs during the match. Novak complained of a hip, upset stomach, and rolled his ankle. Tommy would take exception to this. Tommy thought Novak was taking advantage of the rules using the timeouts for additional rest.

In 2009, Novak would suffer from heat exhaustion in the quarterfinals at the Australian Open. Thus, Novak was not able to successfully to defend his first major title.

Once again, Novak's physical ailments let him down in the 2010 Australian Open. He got stomach aches and vomited on the court. He would eventually lose to Jo Wilfred Tsonga who he defeated to win the 2008 Australian Open.

There were definitely signs of concerns in the Novak camp. Novak seemed to get physically drained, sick, and exhausted. Novak, himself, did not know the reason. Despite the critics, Novak was training hard physically, mentally, and spiritually.

Finally, Novak was approached by a gentleman Dr. Igo Cetojevic. Dr. Cetojevic was able to advise Novak that he was gluten intolerant, and Novak needed to change his diet. It was diagnosed that Novak could no absorb foods with certain wheat and other processed products. As a result, Novak completely changed his diet.

By changing his diet, Novak had one of the greatest years a men's tennis player has ever had in 2011. Novak won the Australian Open defeated Federer in semis and Murray in the finals. Novak won 41 consecutive matches (43 considering Novak had two opponent walkovers).

Novak did not lose his first match until June, when he lost to Federer in the semifinals. Novak came back and won Wimbledon for the first time.

Novak would also capture his first U.S. Open Championship, defeating Roger in the semis and Rafa in the finals. Novak's incredible 2011 would result in an amazing 70-6 record (64-2 at the end of the U.S. Open). He won 10 tournaments. Novak was also 4-1 against Roger and 6-0 against Rafa. Novak was also finishing matches extremely fit and strong as was evidenced in a five hour marathon 2012 Australian Open Final. Novak would defeat Rafa in five intense sets.

From Not Winning The Big One To Becoming A Legend:

After defeating Rafa in the 2012 Australian Open, Novak proved that he was going to be the player to beat. He was on top of the world and would also repeat as the number one player. However, Novak did not dominate like he did in 2011. The other three of the Big Four each won a major in 2012.

What was also happening is Novak would have trouble breaking through and winning majors on a consistent basis like Roger and Rafa did in their dominate years. After the 2012 Australian Open Title, Novak won only one major title in two years. That title he won was the 2013 Australian Open.

Between the 2012 Australian Open and 2014 Wimbledon, he would win one major in six finals appearance. There were questions on Novak being a big match and clutch player. He had so many opportunities to breakthrough, but he could not finish the job. One evidence was the 2013 U.S. Open Final, where Novak was about to go up two sets to one over Nadal. However,

Novak could not hold on to the lead and surrendered the match and his number one ranking to Nadal. Not only did Novak lose twice in the majors to Rafa, he also lost his number one ranking to him.

As a result of not winning multiple majors during this time, Novak hired three time Wimbledon Champion and former number one, Boris Becker as his coach. Marian Vajda would stay on the coaching staff with Boris being the lead coach. Boris' ability to deliver in the big matches would help Novak on the mental side to be relentless when the match got close.

Going into the 2014 Wimbledon, Novak was still among the favorites. Yet, many questioned whether he would be able to lift the trophy. Wimbledon 2014 was a bit of a struggle for Novak. He had to fight off being down two sets to one to Croatia's Marin Cilic in the quarters. Novak was able to come back and advance. He struggled too in the semis against Grigor Dimitrov, but prevailed to make the finals. Roger Federer would be the opponent who was having a great Wimbledon and breezed past Raonic in the other semifinal.

Roger and Novak would battle hard for the first three sets, where Novak took a two sets to one lead. Novak got up 5-2 in the fourth set and appeared to have the match. However, Roger stormed back to take the next five games and win the 4th set 7-5.

It appeared that Novak was going to lose another big match. He had the match on his racquet and relinquished it.

Novak played the fifth more determined than I have even seen him. At 4-5, Roger was serving to stay in the match. Yet, Novak went for the win and captured his 2nd Wimbledon title. This was one of the most epic matches Novak was involved in and showed what a great champion he was. He had defeated Roger on his favorite surface and reclaimed the number one ranking. Novak would finish number one for the year as well.

The best though was ahead as 2015 would be an incredibly special year for Novak. Novak reached heights that no player has been before. Sometimes great tennis players get in a zone where they are unbeatable. 2015 found Novak in this zone all year. As incredible 2011 was, 2015 turned out even better. Unlike 2011, Novak finished 2015 strong. 2015 was just amazing.

Novak would recapture the Australian Open over Andy Murray in the finals. Despite losing in the finals at the French Open, Novak would have one of his best years at Wimbledon. Once again, Novak would face Roger in the finals. The first two sets were both tiebreakers with each taking one. Novak was making Roger work extremely hard, and it paid dividends in the last two sets. Novak would take the racquet out of Roger's hand and successfully defend his Wimbledon title.

The U.S. Open of 2015 would be another major for Novak and his 2nd U.S. Open championship. He defeated Roger in the finals in four sets. The match was pretty much identical to the Wimbledon encounter, where Novak's defense was too much for Roger. It would be his third major in 2015, equaling 2011.

Novak was going up against his great 2011 season. This time though Novak finished the year much stronger. Novak would win his next three tournaments going into the ATP Finals.

Losing in the round robin to Roger snapped his 23 match winning streak. Novak did win his other two round robin matches to qualify for the semifinals. He would easily defeat Rafa in the semifinals and face Roger again in the finals. This time Novak would defeat Roger to capture his fourth consecutive ATP Finals title and his fifth overall.

Novak's 2015 were perhaps the great single season any tennis player has ever had. He had 82 wins 6 losses and 11 titles. He won 3 out of 4 majors and made at least the finals of all four. He won 6 out of 8 Masters 1000 and made the finals in all of them. Novak only failed not to make the finals in only one tournament, which was at the beginning of the year at Doha. It was an incredible year.

Novak picked up in 2016, where he left off in 2015. The 2016 Australian Open brought Novak his 11th major title and 6 Australian Open championships. Once again, he defeated Andy Murray. Novak would also finally breakthrough and win the French Open in 2016 to capture the career Grand Slam. Novak would also win his fourth consecutive major and would be the first men's player to hold all four major titles since Rod Laver accomplished that feat since 1969. It was Nole Slam.

Novak would not only prove that he was a big match player, he would cement his legacy as a legend of the game. Novak would place himself as one of the greatest players to ever play the game of tennis. Novak would accomplish being a legend by overcoming adversity time and time again. The biggest obstacle was yet to come.

Injury, Burnout, and Return to Number One:

In June of 2016, Novak Djokovic conquered to one feat in tennis that was eluding him, winning the French Open. Once Novak became the French Open Champion, he had accomplished everything anyone could in the game of tennis. Not only had he won all four majors, Novak became the first men's player since Rod Laver in 1969 to win four consecutive majors. Novak was on top of the world and was unstoppable. Maybe the only person that could defeat Novak was perhaps Novak himself.

Novak had single handedly dominated the men's tour in 2015 and was doing the same during the first half of 2016. Many were talking about Novak winning the calendar Grand Slam, and now that was possible with the French Open title. It seemed like the only one who could stop Novak was Novak himself.

Something was going on in Novak that very few knew about. He did withdraw in a tournament early in 2016 with an elbow problem. Yet, people did not know what was going on inside of

Novak. Novak was feeling the pressure to win week in and week out, and it finally got to him. That 2016 French Open victory was more of a relief and an exciting time for Novak. Novak had hit an emotional wall and completely burned out. There was something missing for Novak, especially when he questions himself, "this is it?" after accomplishment everything on the court, but not being fulfilled.

At Wimbledon 2016 and holding all four majors, the onion began to unpeel. Yet, the public thought it was just a minor setback due to injury. Novak was knocked out in the third round and was unable to defend his title. Many thought Novak would come back and win the Open. Things appeared to be okay when Novak won a big tournament in Toronto later that summer. However, the Olympic Gold Medal eluded Novak once again, when he was upset by Argentina's Juan Martin Del Potro. A teary eyed Novak would leave the court knowing that his quest for Gold was not yet fulfilled.

As the U.S. Open arrived, Novak had thought about withdrawing due to the elbow injury. Novak would have two walkovers and also played two opponents in the draw that had put in little effort in their matches in Jo-Wilfred Tsonga and Gael Monfils. Novak would face a very hungry Stan Wawrinka in the finals. Stan was a very talented and heavy ball striking player who matched up against Novak extremely well. Both had great battles, and Stan had beaten Novak twice in a big matches. Novak was not playing his best tennis. Yet, he found himself in the finals and won the first set. However, Stan looked like the player who wanted it more. As a result, Stan won the next three sets to dethrone Novak.

During the fall, Novak appeared listless in a couple tournaments. He even stated to the media that chasing Roger Federer's record of 17 majors was not a priority. Novak also hired a spiritual guru in his camp, as he would look to him for spiritual guidance.

Regardless, his ability was getting him deep in tournaments and got to the finals at the ATP Finals. However, he would lose the match and his number one ranking to Andy Murray. Despite the ongoing elbow injury, the second half of 2016 was clearly underwhelming for Novak.

As 2017 approached, it appeared that Novak would return to top form and win his 4th consecutive Australian Open title. However, he was upset in the second round. It was apparent that Novak was still not ready to compete at a high level. During this time too, Novak had let go of one his coaches, Boris Becker.

After the Australian Open, Novak would then let go of his long-time coach Marian Vajda. Vajda developed Novak and was there for all those wins. Now he was gone. Novak was also following the guidance of his spiritual guru.

Novak went into the French Open to defend his title not winning a tournament in 2017. He had just hired American tennis legend Andre Agassi as his new coach. After leading 4-2 in the first set in the quarterfinals, Novak would go on to lose the first set. Novak then lost the two remaining sets to Domenic Thiem and get dethroned. Novak appeared unraveled on the court. His great two handed backhand was breaking down, and he seemed in a hurry to get off the court.

Wimbledon saw Novak withdraw in the quarterfinals due to the persistent elbow injury. At this point, the elbow injury had been going on for 18 months. At that point, it seemed that it was time to shut it down for a while. Shortly after, Novak announced that he was going to sit out for the remainder of the year and heal the elbow.

2018 was a new beginning for Novak. He added Radek Stepanek to the coaching staff that already consisted of Agassi. Many thought Novak would was ready to go, despite the fact he was coming off injury. For the Australian Open, expectations were not too high. Novak had to tweak his serve due to the elbow. Novak would lose in the fourth round. What was surprising though is the elbow injury continued to persist. Novak decided not to have surgery. Experts were stating that Novak should have gotten the right people to properly rehabilitate the elbow.

Finally after the Australian Open, Novak decided to have surgery. Novak rehabilitated for the remainder of the winter and played some tournaments in the spring, where naturally he did not look sharp losing early and often. Yet, the best thing happened during this time. Novak would part ways with Agassi and Stepanek as his coaches. Novak also let go of his spiritual guru. Novak, then, rehired Marian Vajda as his coach and his old staff.

At this time though, the fans and media were writing Novak off. Questions on the constant switching and his movement were in play. Many thought Novak was washed up and did not have it anymore. During these times, Novak even questioned himself. Those questions were even brought up again when Novak lost in the quarters at the French Open.

Going into Wimbledon that summer, no one gave Novak a chance to win it. Yet, Novak began to find his form in the third round. Novak then found himself getting to the semifinals facing Rafael Nadal who was one of the favorites to win. A two day epic semifinal saw Novak win in a tight five set thriller. The fifth set was 10-8 and showed Novak still had the ability to deliver when it truly mattered. Novak would then to go on and win the finals against South Africa's Kevin Anderson to recapture glory and a Wimbledon title. All of a sudden Novak was dialed in and ready to compete at the highest level.

Novak would go on and have a solid summer and won his 3rd

U.S. Open title and 14th major title overall, tying him with Pete Sampras for third place. All of a sudden, Novak went from being a has-been to winning back to back majors and an opportunity to finish the year at # 1.

Novak would have a solid fall season and reclaimed his number one ranking. He was also playing his best tennis ever and enjoying it. Novak would go into 2019 reaffirming his number one ranking recapturing the Australian Open. It would be his 7th Australian Open title as he easily defeated 2nd ranked Nadal.

Of all the adversity Novak has to overcome, I believe that these last few years had to be the toughest climb for him. Novak had been tested physically, mentally, emotionally, and spiritually in more ways than one. Very few could have overcome what Novak has had. Yet, Novak's courage has proven that he can go from rock bottom to the top of the world and become one the greatest tennis players of all time.

WHAT WE CAN LEARN FROM NOVAK DJOKOVIC

N ot only is Novak Djokovic one of the greatest tennis players of all-time, he is also remarkable for his openness about the trials and tribulations that have affected his life. He has displayed a willingness to share his life and truth with fans. What do I mean by that? If you took all the advice that he shares and put together a self-development book, it would be a best-seller. Djokovic's approach of higher-conscious living seems to be a direct product of the adversity he has experienced on and off the court. Novak Djokovic clearly has many lessons to teach us.

Dealing with Fear:

The first lesson I believe that we can take away from Djokovic is how to thrive in the face of fear. He and his family had life and death experiences regularly during his childhood and he described the irony of having so much fear that eventually it went away. There was a freedom that came with being so over-whelmed by his circumstances that he could not change, that he had no control over, and it allowed him to deal with the task at hand. In a sense, he had become fearless.

Djokovic still seems to incorporate this management of fear into his life on and off the tennis court. His tennis game consists of swinging freely for the fences as well as taking risks no other player on tour would take. Even in high-stakes situations, he employs this strategy of fearlessness. For example, down match point against Roger Federer during the 2011 U.S. Open he was undaunted and turned that game around and went on to win the match and eventually the tournament.

If someone like Novak can stop being afraid and live freely during war time, then we can stop living in fear and live freer and be ourselves in our everyday lives. What would you do if you felt free, fearless, and knew you could not fail? How would you pursue your career or your relationships knowing that you could be free regardless of what happens? Would you mind open to new and creative ideas that you could bring to your employer or the market place? Would you be willing to try new things in a relationship? Could thinking and being outside of the box be a new reality?

I remember a great example of being free when I read "The Go Giver" by Bob Burg and John D. Mann. There was a Real Estate Brokers who was failing and was about to throw in the towel to pursue another career opportunity. She knew she was going to leave, but she had one more house to show. Since she knew she was leaving, her mind was free and clear. As a result, she got the sale because she was herself and not worried or stressed. She then realized that being in this mindset of fearlessness and freedom was the key to success for her. She decided to give real estate a second chance. As a result of this change in approach, she became a top-producing real estate broker earning over $1 million per year in commissions.[3]

We can do the things we want to do and be who we want without fear interfering just like Djokovic has done. Remember, his approach doesn't completely erase the fear, but it asks you to look past it as a given- something that you do not have control over. When you recognize you have no control over the circumstance you are required to then move on and put your energies toward the things that you DO have control over. This shift from worry to action is a powerful change you can make.

Love:

During the time that Novak was experiencing his slump he was mentally in a tough place. There was a period of two-and-a half years where he experienced a major championship drought. Fortunately for Djokovic, a close friend confided in him and asked if he still loved the game. Did he still love stepping onto the court, practicing, and playing a match? Did he still love the process?

This friend told Novak to forget about the results and just play for the love of the game. Once Djokovic was able to realize that he still loved to play the game and anything going forward that he achieved would be secondary to that joy. This was a significant realization for Djokovic that freed him from expectation and reintroduced an ease to his game. Unsurprisingly, with this change in mindset, his career went north, he regained his winning form, and became the number one player in the world shortly thereafter.

Love is one of the best methods to deal with adversity. Loving what you do or finding the love in what you do will help you overcome the tough times and deal with the adversity. There is no successful person in this world that does not do what they love to some degree. Finding your love for the process is the most certain way to achieve the results you desire.

Keeping an Open Mind:

Another great way to overcome adversity and learn from Novak Djokovic is to have an open mind. If you're mind is shut, you will lose your shirt. You will lose your business. You will lose your relationship. You will lose your spirit and health as well.

There were two times in Novak's career where an open mind truly paid off for him. The first time was in 2010, where he also was able to recapture the love of the game.

The first time in Novak's career came in late 2010, when Dr. Igo Cetojevic approached Novak on why his body was breaking down during matches. Novak was doing everything to make sure he wasn't breaking down during matches. There were reports that Novak was not fit enough. Yet, Novak was working tremendously hard on his conditioning. Novak would also meditate and have other spiritual practices as well.

Dr. Cetojevic was able to diagnose that Novak was able to process wheat and other foods that were heavy in starch and sugar. Hence, Novak was "gluten intolerant". Thus, Novak's new diet propelled him to lose 10 pounds, which made him much more light and agile on the court.

Had it not been for the "gluten intolerant" diagnosis, Novak would probably never had the season he did in 2011. Novak definitely would not have ever outlasted Rafa in the 2012 Australian Open Finals.

The second time where Novak's open mind paid off was at the end of 2013. After the great 2011 and the Australian Open win in 2012, Novak was still at the top of the game. However, he only won one major for the remaining of 2012 and 2013. Novak was getting to the finals or semifinals, but would find himself on the losing end. Granted the men's field was strong, but Novak was losing big matches on a consistent basis. Novak's coaching staff was intact. Yet, Novak was willing to add a member to the team that was already strong. That person was three time Wimbledon Champion, Hall of Famer Boris Becker. Boris' game when he was playing was very different from Novak's. Boris was an aggressive serve and volley player who relied heavily on offense. Granted Novak could play offensive tennis, but he was much more known as a defensive player who relied on speed and forcing his opponents to come up with the error. Boris would add a little more offense to Novak's superior defensive skills. In addition, Boris had played many big matches in big moments. Thus, he would be able to provide Novak with big match preparation.

Going into the 2014 Wimbledon, Novak had lost 8 of the last 9 majors played. It had been over a year since his last major victory, the 2013 Australian Open.

It appeared that Novak was going to lose again, when he let a 5-2 lead in the 4th set get away. He was playing arguably one of the greatest grass court players in Roger Federer. Once Roger brought the match to a 5th set, it appeared Roger had the momentum. However, working with Boris prepared Novak for these moments. Novak would go on to take the 5th set and the Wimbledon title.

Novak, under Becker, would go onto even surpass 2011 in 2015 where he would not only win 3 majors. He appeared in all 4 major finals. He only failed once not to make a final in every tournament he played in 2015. In 2015, Novak did not fizzle at the end of the year, unlike 2011. In addition, Novak would become the first player since Rod Laver in 1969 to win four consecutive majors with the 2015 Wimbledon and U.S. Open as well as the 2016 Australian and French Open. It was the "Novak Slam".

As we see with Novak, being open minded opens up new possibilities. We saw how a "gluten free" diet gave Novak the stamina to complete long matches and become the number one player in the world. We also saw how hiring an outsider into a successful team can turn around an image of not winning the big matches. Novak was winning big matches and completely dominating men's tennis.

We also have seen what an open mind can have with athletes. Tiger Woods was already a successful golfer in the late 90's. Yet,

Tiger was advised to change his golf swing. Tiger did change his swing and dominated the PGA tour. Even Roger Federer finally relented to switch to a lighter racquet. As a result, Roger's backhand became a weapon and won two majors in 2017 after nearly a five year drought.

We have seen how an open minded person can fail at trying to invent a glue that would permanently stick. After the failure, he was open to see what he could do with the substance and created the "post it note".

I have seen how an open mind created great things in my life, especially in my relationship with my wife as well as me getting involved in self-development.

Lastly, we can learn from Novak and overcome adversity with Novak's practice of a high conscious living. One is to find your purpose, so you can help others find theirs. Novak also believes that happiness is from the inside. In addition, happiness and inner peace is the ultimate goal. The inner peace enabled Novak to finish number one in the world four out of five years. The inner peace also enabled him to go inside of himself when the outside world was not for him. An example was the 2015 U.S. Open Final against Roger. Besides his team and a few others, the entire stadium was rooting for Roger. When Novak heard "Go Roger" or "Come on Roger" he was able to internalize and envision that the crowd was chanting "Go Nole" and "Come on Nole". Novak would have to go against the crowd many times when he was against Roger and Rafa.

Having a holistic practice made him overcome these deficits and have an overall career winning record against both Roger and Rafa as I presently write this.

Just Breathe:

Novak defines hatred and revenge as prisoners of their own emotions. Lastly, Novak believes in the power of breathing so that we can stay in the present.

Novak's three truths are to live freely, breathe deeply, and love fully.

With a spiritual practice like Novak's we can prosper in all areas of our lives. Being present will able to have fuller and healthier lives. One way is to appreciate food and eat it consciously bite after bite.

Living freely will add value to other making us much more abundant not only financially, but more important emotionally and spiritually. We see this on how joyous whether Novak is with a ball girl or boy or laughing it up with his peers during practices and exhibitions.

Love fully has played a huge part of Novak's life with his appreciation for his wife, connection with his fans, and being a goodwill ambassador to UNICEF (provide humanitarian and developmental assistance to children).

Thus if we apply living fully to our careers like Novak, we can add tremendous value in the marketplace. We have plenty of great role models like Richard Branson, Bill Gates, or Oprah Winfrey. All three add tremendous value to others in our society and are very rich because of that.

Breathing can be accomplished through any practice like yoga or meditation. It is important to live in the moment so we can catch everything around us and have great relationships. Living in the present enables you to excel at your craft like Novak does on the tennis court. It also creates joy and makes everyday a holiday.

2012 AUSTRALIAN OPEN MEN'S FINAL

When it comes to epic finals matches, 2012 Australian Open final between Novak Djokovic and Rafael Nadal ranks among the most exciting ever played. The two competitors went to battle on the tennis court for almost 6 grueling hours, making it the longest final ever played. The performance by Djokovic will be remembered as one of his greatest, not only for his ability to win against another championship-pedigree player in Nadal, but because in the semifinal he played 5 sets against Andy Murray in another match that lasted 5 hours. Djokovic's ability to play 2 matches of that difficulty back-to-back display his composure and talent when faced with challenges.

Going into the match, Novak Djokovic was facing the pressures that come along with success on the tour. For the first time he was no longer hunting down the top players, he was the hunted. Djokovic was the defending tournament champion with his Australian Open win in 2011 and in the process became the number one player in the world. He now had a target on his back.

There was also added pressure from the fact that despite having a breakthrough year, Djokovic did not finish strong in 2011.

After winning the first major of that year, he did not win another tournament in 2011. In fact, it was Roger Federer who regained his form and won in Paris and the ATP Finals.

Lastly, his opponent in the final was Nadal. Rafael Nadal loved to be the hunter, and because Nadal was 0 for 6 against Novak in 2011, he very much wanted to even the score in 2012. Nadal was gunning for a physically depleted Novak Djokovic who already played 5 hours of demanding tennis against Andy Murray in the semis. This was a highly anticipated matchup with a great amount of hype surrounding it. It was the two best players in the world at the time ready to do battle. Their matches were known to be heavyweight fights. Both players play an extremely physical game with power and unmatched speed.

In the start of first set, the two players were feeling each other out in the style of a chess match. Nadal had clearly come into the match prepared to address his shortcomings that resulted in six head-to-head losses against Djokovic. As was expected after his long semi-final match against Murray, Djokovic was a little slow moving out of the gates trying to get into a rhythm. Nadal capitalized on this and drew first blood. With Djokovic serving at 2-2, Nadal was able to break his serve by hitting a magnificent cross court shot past Djokovic who was positioned to volley.

Losing his serve seemed to awaken Djokovic. He started to go to work on Nadal's serve, hitting a couple of deep returns. However, Nadal managed to hold on to his service game and go up 4 games to 2. In the next game Djokovic did hold strong on his serve although he couldn't shake the sluggishness. With Nadal up 4-3 and serving, Djokovic put the pressure on with each return and ended up breaking back to tie the set at 4 games all. Even though Nadal was playing aggressively, and Djokovic wasn't playing at the top of his game, the match was even.

Djokovic managed to hold to make it 5-4, but Nadal held as well by hitting another remarkable cross court forehand. With Djokovic serving at 5--all, Nadal hit a beautiful down the line fore-hand that was pure brilliance. Djokovic hit an unforced error and Nadal earned his second break of the set to go up 6-5.

At 6-5 it was another close game. Yet with Nadal playing much more of an offensive game, he was able to take the first set 7-5.

Djokovic now seemed to have his back against the wall. This was not the same Nadal he had seen in the previous Wimble-don and U.S. Open. How was Djokovic going to respond to this challenge? After an exchange of holds, Djokovic is the one who initiated an attack by breaking Nadal to go up 3-1. Djokovic was definitely looking fresher and sharper. Djokovic holds to go up 4-1 with that game ending in a beautiful drop shot. Djokovic was beginning to make Nadal work very hard on the serve. He was also beginning to take control of the match, playing it more on his terms. At 5-2 with Nadal serving, Djokovic hit an incred-ible stretch backhand return winner. Nadal did manage to hold to make it 5-3. With Djokovic serving for the set, Nadal fought and managed to break back with Djokovic serving a double fault. However, Nadal returned the favor by doubling faulting on his serve and Djokovic broke back to take the second set 6-4.

In the third set, at 2-1, Djokovic broke Nadal to go up 3-1. With beautiful ground strokes and taking command Djokovic then easily held to go up 4-1. Djokovic was relentless pressuring Nadal's serve, especially on the second serve. Even when Nadal was holding, Djokovic would get the games to deuce and get break point opportunities. After an exchange of breaks, it was 5-2 Djokovic. With Nadal serving at 5-2, Djokovic hit a massive forehand winner to break at love and win the set 6-2. Third set to Djokovic. He took command of the match and had one more set to go.

At the start of the fourth set, it seemed like Djokovic just needed to continue to do what he was doing the last two sets. He seemed to have overcome the charging Nadal and it was more of the same as 2011.

With his back against the wall, Nadal was a little more aggressive to start the fourth set going more for his shots. Both players held serve in the first two games, but both games were tight. Nadal stayed much firmer this time as the level of play has picked up and both are going at each other. Still on serve at 4-3, Nadal was serving and appeared to get in trouble again. At 0-30, Nadal is desperate as he hits a tremendous cross court forehand. The only thing Novak is able to get is a slice backhand but does and gets it down the line which baffles Nadal. Nadal manages to get it back, but it is an easy put away for Djokovic. Now it is 0-40. Djokovic is 5 points away from winning his third Australian Open title. At 0-40, Nadal saves one breakpoint with a forehand winner. At 15-40, Nadal gets an ace. Then at 30-40, stays alive with a backhand winner down the line. And just that quickly the game score is at deuce. Nadal wins the next two points with an ace and a Novak return in the net. It is 4-4, and Nadal has escaped for the time being.

At 4-4, there is a momentary delay as the rain comes and the arena roof needs to be closed. Once play resumes, both players hold to make It 5-5. Both players are making unbelievable exchanges as Nadal has clearly raised his level and is fighting to stay alive. At 5-all, Djokovic holds to make it 6-5. Nadal does not blink though, making it 6-6. It is time for a tiebreaker.

Djokovic serves first in the tiebreaker and holds to make it 1-0. Nadal, on his own serve, hits another killer forehand making Djokovic just miss the volley, 1-1. Nadal holds again to go up 2-1. Djokovic makes it 2-2, but Nadal gets the mini break to go up 3-2 on a Djokovic unforced error. Back to 3-3 when Nadal clips the net and the ball sails out.

The players cross over sides at 3-3. Once play resumes Djokovic breaks Nadal again to go up 4-3 and then hits a forehand winner to go up 5-3. Two points away from the finish line.

Nadal fights back again with a mini break off of an incredible exchange that finished with a wide forehand by Djokovic. The two players get a well-deserved standing ovation from the fans. Back on serve at 5-5, Djokovic hits an unforced error into the net. Nadal is digging in deep and so isn't allowing Djokovic to finish this. Nadal hits a big first serve to Djokovic's forehand that goes wide, 6-5 set point Nadal. At 6-5, Nadal hits a forehand winner to take the fourth set 7-6. Fourth set to Nadal. Nadal has come back from the dead to bring the match to a fifth set. Djokovic would need to respond to Nadal's challenge and dig deep to win this.

As the fifth set is about to begin, it was apparent that this would be a massive test of Djokovic's fitness. In the past Djokovic was known to collapse and fizzle out. So there was speculation as to whether Djokovic would be able to keep up his play against the physically fit Nadal? Nadal served first and both players hold to make it 1-1.

Nadal holds at love to make it 2-1. Djokovic holds to make it 2-all but struggles to do so. Djokovic's legs are tightening. Nadal holds at love to make it 3-2 as Djokovic looks to be conserving energy as well. For the first time since the first set, Nadal breaks Djokovic for a 4-2 lead. At 4-2 Nadal tries to consolidate the break by holding at 30-15. Nadal missed an easy backhand down the line and the ball goes out. Naturally frustrated by the easy miss he challenges the call. However, it is a desperate challenge and call stands. It is 30 all. That gives Djokovic a little momentum back and crushes a backhand cross court. At break point and Djokovic converts to get back on serve, 4-3. Djokovic holds, and it is 4-4. At 4-4, the first point was another incredibly long rally where Djokovic hits a shot that sails long. Djokovic battled to get a breakpoint opportunity, but once again Nadal held, 5-4. Djokovic held too to make it 5-5.

At 5-all and Nadal serving, Nadal hits a stretching beautiful forehand to go down the line, 15-0. It would get to 30-30 when Djokovic hits a deep forehand that Nadal sails into the net, 30-40 break point. Nadal would get the game back to deuce. Djokovic would earn another break point and this time he converts the break to go up 6-5.

Djokovic is now serving for the championship. He gets up 30-0, but Nadal wins the next two points. He then earned a break point after an unbelievable display of defense where he forced Nadal to make an error. It was absolutely incredible, and Djokovic was able to get back to deuce.

Novak would earn his first championship point when Nadal clipped the net and went out, advantage Djokovic. Djokovic then served with a return from Rafa that turned into an easy winner for Djokovic and that sealed the Australian Open Championship. This was the third and most difficult Australian Open title for Djokovic. He would hug Nadal and then the adrenaline took over as he rips his shirt and greeted his team. It was an unbelievable and incredible match, one of the greatest matches ever.

During the trophy presentation ceremony both players were so completely drained and exhausted that the official brought out chairs and water for the two. Nadal and Djokovic would go on to have future success and great match ups with each other, but to this day, the Australian Open final is arguably their greatest match against each other and was a defining moment for Djokovic.

Djokovic dug deep like he never did before and proved to have a warrior-like toughness to match Nadal's tenacity. Novak Djokovic had won at this test of wills. This was the longest major final ever played and the match put Djokovic at another level. He defended his title against one of the toughest opponents and against immense pressure.

TENACITY
RAFAEL NADAL

TENACITY

"The glory is being happy. The glory is not winning here or winning there. The glory is to enjoy practicing, enjoy every day, enjoy working hard, trying to be a better player than before."

"Losing is not my enemy. Fear of losing is my enemy."

- Rafael Nadal

Out of the big four, it can be argued that no one brings the intensity, passion, and tenacity that Rafael "Rafa" Nadal does. Rafa is often cited as one of the hardest working tennis players on the circuit if ever. Tennis legend John McEnroe has said that not even his old rival Jimmy Connors played with as much fire as Rafa. Rafa plays every single point like it is his last. He plays with pure passion and grit. Every opponent knows that when they go up against Rafa, they will need to put in their best effort or they will lose the match severely.

Known as the 'King of Clay," Rafa has dominated the clay courts like no one before him. He holds virtually all the clay court records one can have including 11 French Open titles. Only Margaret Court at the Australian Open can match Rafa's 11 titles in one major. Yet, unlike many other clay court specialists, Rafa has excelled on all surfaces.

Rafael Nadal is the only lefty out of the big four. He is known as a defensive player and counter puncher. In some ways, he has revolutionized the game for players who play on the baseline and whose game relies on defense. His heavy topspin, which he can hit at 90 miles per hour (mph) and 3200 revolutions per minute (rpm) has set him apart from the other elite players. Like Novak Djokovic, Nadal is able to hit all angles with precision. His great speed allows him to run down anything on the court, so opponents know they always need to be ready to hit that extra ball that comes back to them. Nadal's intensity forces his opponents to make errors.

The drawback to Nadal's all-out aggressive style is the number of injuries that he has endured throughout his illustrious career. He has had to battle injuries to his knee, foot, back, abdomen, and wrist. These injuries have resulted in many setbacks and extended time off. However, the injuries have never kept him from achieving great things. Rafa is a fighter and after each injury, he has come back even stronger and more determined.

Early Childhood:

Rafael Nadal Parera was born June 3, 1986 on the Balearic Islands of Spain in the city of Manacor to parents Sebastian Nadal and Ana Maria Parera. His father is a successful businessman with various ventures including a window manufacturer, insurance company, restaurant, and café.

The Nadal's have always been a very close and tight-knit family. Rafa has two siblings: his brother Tomeu Nadal and his sister Maria Isabel Nadal. To this day, the family all live close together in an apartment complex they own. From a young age, the children were instilled with values of hard work, respect for others, and humility. Throughout his career, Rafa has demonstrated these traits on and off the court.

At the age 4, Rafa picked up a racquet and right away the Nadal family took notice of Rafa's talent. Sebastian had two brothers,

Miguel and Toni, who were professional athletes and they identified their young nephew's talent immediately. Miguel was a professional soccer player and had played for Spain in the 2002 World Cup. Toni was a top-30 tennis player and part-time tennis coach. 'Uncle Toni' began working with Rafa full time to develop the boy's talent. The family supported this move and Sebastian and Miguel minded their brother's interest in the family business, so he could dedicate 100% of his focus to training Rafa.

Training With Uncle Toni:

At a young age, Rafa was training five times a week. By age 12, Rafa was so skilled that he could play with both hands. Uncle Toni convinced Rafa to play left-handed as it would give him an advantage and keep his opponents off balance. Aside from the technical parts of the game, Uncle Toni also wanted to ensure that his nephew learned the fundamentals of fair play and conduct as a sportsperson. Toni told Rafa to never smash or break a tennis racquet. He made it clear that if Rafa were to ever smash a racquet, he would no longer be his coach. In Rafa's biography, it was explained that smashing a racquet would be showing a lack of respect to people who must buy equipment to play the sport as well as to those who could not afford one.

Uncle Toni also had some unconventional training methods. He used to train Rafa on bad courts with bad tennis balls and windy conditions. The original intent was to teach Rafa that winning was not about the quality of the courts, strings, and weather conditions, but it was about attitude, discipline, and perspective. The training not only paid off for Rafa's pro career, but it also gave Rafa a decisive advantage against his opponents during tough weather conditions.

Rafa would win his share of junior tournaments, and Uncle Toni always made sure Rafa would remain humble. Toni reminded Rafa of the slim possibilities of becoming a pro tennis player and continue to work hard. Toni also reminded Rafa that he is in control of his destiny.

The hard work and tenacity that Rafa displays would come from Uncle Toni and the values of the Nadal family. To this day at practice, Rafa picks up his own tennis balls and sweeps the clay courts himself.

A Young Star Ready To Breakthrough:

Unlike many of his talented counterparts, Rafa remained in Mallorca instead of going to a training academy in Barcelona or America. It was believed that Toni was doing a good enough job coaching.

One early indicator that Rafa was going to be great was at age 14 when he defeated former Wimbledon Champion Pat Cash in an exhibition match. Pat Cash was 35 and retired from the tour. However, Pat was still in great tennis shape playing on the men's senior tour.

Rafael's junior tour was brief as he turned pro in 2001 at the age of 15. At that time, Spain was making its presence felt on the men's tour. Mostly known as a country that produces clay court specialists, many of Spain's tennis exports began to show range on all surfaces. It was as if the evolution of these players was leading the path for Nadal.

In the 1970's, Manuel Orantes won the U.S. Open when it was still a clay surface. There was also Sergi Bruguera who won back-to-back French Open titles in 1993 and 1994. After Sergi, it was like a wave of new talent came in from Spain. Alex Corretja was an extremely gifted player on all surfaces, but his best surface was clay. Then there was fellow player, and later coach, Carlos Moya. Moya would defeat Corretja at the 1998 French Open final. Moya also was a finalist at the 1997 Australian Open. Moya would later go on to coach Rafa.

In addition, there was 2002 French Open champion Albert

Costa as well as a 2003 French Open Champion Juan Carlos Fer-rero (also known as "The Mosquito.") Ferrero, like Moya and Corretja, showed success on other surfaces and appeared to be headed for greatness until injuries came along and another young player named Roger Federer started to cement his own legendary career.

Spain would win the 2000 Davis Cup with the crew of Moya, Ferrero, Costa, and Corretja. They were deep with talent and building a dynasty. Once Rafa came along, there were rumors that Rafa was going to take the torch to be the best player in Spain and win the French Open. Yet, many had absolutely no idea what was to come- how many French titles he and how many other majors he would win as well. No one could possibly imagine what a humble, shy, and hardworking kid from the is-land of Mallorca would come to accomplish.

RAFA'S TENACITY AND PASSION

Competing With The Best

W hen Rafael Nadal came onto the scene, he wasn't ne-cessarily singled-out to become one of the greatest players of all-time. He was clearly an heir-apparent to the proud Spanish tennis dynasty- the same ilk of a Moya and Ferrero. It was safe to say he would likely win a French Open or two. But it was hard to fathom that he would eventually win 11 of those titles as well as complete a career Grand Slam of win-ning each of the 3 other majors.

In 2003, a teenage Rafa earned a spot to play in two Grand Slam tournaments- Wimbledon and the U.S. Open. It was defeated in the 3rd and 2nd round respectively.

The year that people began to really take notice of Rafael Nadal was 2004 when he upset Roger Federer in the Miami Open. Roger had only lost one match out of these last 28 matches. Soon after, during the Davis Cup Finals against the United States, Nadal faced-off against Andy Roddick in the singles. In a previous meeting between the two at the U.S. Open, Roddick had annihi-lated Nadal. This was Nadal's turn to get revenge and he did so by beating Roddick 6-7(6), 6-3, 7-6(6), 6-2. After that match, the tennis community was on notice that this 18-year old would be a serious contender at every tournament.

The momentum he had built in the previous year carried into a breakout 2005 where Nadal went from a rank of 151 in the world to #2 at the end of 2005. He started 2005 pushing Lleyton Hewitt to 5 sets in the 4th round of the Australian Open. He then went on to win clay tournaments in Sao Paulo and Acapulco. In Miami, he found himself facing Federer again- but this time in the finals. In this match, Nadal surrendered an early two set lead to lose to Federer in 5 sets.

After Nadal suffered a surprising loss at clay tournament in Valencia, he recovered from this stumble to win his first Masters 1000 in Monte Carlo, defeating Guillermo Coria. Rafa then won in Barcelona over Ferrero and won in Rome over Coria once again. He was becoming an unstoppable force on clay.

Roland Garros:

Going into Roland Garros, Rafa was the favorite to win his first major. He had to get by Roger in the semis and did so in 4 sets. Argentina's Mariano Puerta was Rafa's opponent in the finals.

After losing a tiebreaker in the 1st set, Rafa took the next three sets and won his first major. It was a momentous occasion that capped of an incredible clay court season for the 19-year old Nadal. It didn't take long for Nadal to capture that first Grand Slam, but that didn't mean the rest of the road as smooth sailing.

In the very next Grand Slam tournament at Wimbledon, Nadal crashed out in a second-round loss. However, once he returned to clay he would display the form that that everyone was used to, winning in both Sweden and Germany.

Rafa would win his first hard court Masters 1000 defeating Agassi in the finals in Montreal. But he couldn't translate that to success in the U.S. Open and lost to James Blake of the United States in the third round.

A few weeks later, Nadal did win in Beijing and he would win another Masters 1000 by defeating Ivan Ljubicic in 5 sets at the then indoor tournament in Madrid. Despite the stellar year that he had, Rafa would not play the ATP Finals due to injury. He had a record of 79-10, eleven titles, one major, four Masters 1000 titles, and a #2 ranking in the world.

2006 saw Rafa continue to progress by upholding an undefeated record on clay, including defeating Federer in the French Open Finals to capture his second straight championship at that tournament. There was also a five-set thriller at the Rome Masters finals, where he defeated Federer 6-7(0), 7-6 (5), 6-4, 2-6, 7-6(5). Adding to his impressive run that year was an appearance in the Wimbledon final, where he would ultimately lose to his rival Roger Federer 6-0, 7-6(5), 6-7 (2), 6-3.

By the end of the 2006 tennis season, Rafa finished #2 in the world and was 4-2 in head-to-head match-ups against Roger Federer. Rafa's record in 2006 was 59-12. He won five titles, and two Masters 1000 titles.

Domination:

Nadal continued his high level of play throughout the 2007 season. He won his third-straight French Open title and was virtually unbeatable on the clay. His only loss on clay came at the hands of Federer at Hamburg and was a continuation of their sensational rivalry. He bested Federer in four sets in the French Open finals rematch; but came up short against Federer in the Wimbledon final- a five set thriller. By the end of the 2007 season Rafa would finish with a 70-15 win/loss record which included 6 titles, three Masters 1000 titles, his third-straight French Open title, and holding his place at the #2 ranking. The year was a great one for him but 2008 would be even more special.

His year started with an excellent showing at the Australian Open by reaching the semi-finals. Later in the year he would also reach the semis at the U.S. Open. His level of play across all surfaces was starting to lift. He still dominated on clay by winning in Monte Carlo, Hamburg, and Barcelona. Unsurprisingly he captured his fourth-consecutive French Open title by crushing Federer 6-1, 6-3, 6-0. It was Federer's worst defeat and this would become especially significant going into the Wimbledon finals where they would face-off against each other yet again.

The 2008 Wimbledon Men's Final is considered by many to be the greatest match ever played. Nadal won the first two sets and somehow Federer fought back taking tiebreakers in both the third and fourth sets. This collapse was especially disheartening for Nadal because he had a match point while serving in the in the fourth-set tiebreaker only to surrender it and lose 10-8. It took five sets for Nadal to put away the match. With this epic match, Nadal earned his first Wimbledon and later in the summer would go on to take the #1 ranking from Federer who had held it for 4 ½ straight years.

Going from strength to strength, Rafa also won the Olympic Gold Medal in Beijing for the men's singles in 2008.

A Rough Patch:

The 2009 tennis season started off the right foot for Nadal. He won his first hard court major capturing the Australian Open title defeating Roger Federer in five sets. There was a special moment at the trophy ceremony where Nadal was consoled an emotional Federer.

Nadal would win at Indian Wells and then take care of business on clay winning Monte Carlo, Barcelona, and Rome. Madrid was a different story. He won an incredible semifinal match against Djokovic 3-6, 7-6(5), 7-6(9). This taxing win appeared to take a toll on Nadal and he lost in the semifinals to Federer.

At the time, the Madrid loss appeared to be a minor setback, however Nadal would then go on to suffer his first ever loss at the French Open. He lost to Sweden's Robin Soderling in the fourth round. It was a perfect storm of Nadal being less than 100% and Soderling playing a brilliantly aggressive game plan that took the match to the reigning champion.

The year didn't get any easier for Nadal as he was unable to defend his Wimbledon title- withdrawing due to a knee injury. Nadal did recover in time to get back to the summer hard court season earning a semifinal appearance at Cincinnati. He made the semifinals at the U.S. Open, but succumbed to an abdominal strain. As a result, Juan Martin Del Potro easily defeated Nadal 6-2, 6-2, 6-2. Del Potro would go on to win his first major at the tournament.

After a great start to the year, Nadal did not win a tournament after April.

The Comeback:

It wasn't until the clay tournaments the following year, in 2010 that Nadal began to find his form again. He won all three Masters 1000 clay tournaments, then captured his 5th French Open title avenging his 2009 loss to Robin Soderling in the finals 6-4, 6-2, 6-4.

The two would meet at Wimbledon as well, with Nadal defeating Soderling at the quarters and winning in 4 sets. Nadal recaptured the Wimbledon title by defeating Berdych 6-3, 7-5, 6-4 in the finals. With two majors wins in 2010, he had his eyes set on adding the U.S. Open to his resume.

Nadal entered the U.S. Open tournament as the #1 seed. Going into the semifinals Nadal had not lost a set. This time the opponent was Russia's Mikhail Youzhny. Nadal would prevail and make his first U.S. Open Final. He would face the dangerous Novak Djokovic in the finals. Novak played a tough match against Nadal, but Nadal was not going to be denied. He would capture his first U.S. Open title and the career slam.

Nadal finished the 2010 season with three Masters 1000 titles, seven titles, three majors, and he regained the #1 ranking. This was Nadal's best season to-date.

A New Rivalry:

In 2011, Nadal would play some great tennis. However, he would run into an obstacle in the form of Novak Djokovic. Djokovic had his first huge year and went 6-0 against Nadal. Djokovic's defense and backhand down the line was a difficult matchup for Nadal, even on clay.

Nadal was destroying everyone else on the tour in 2011 except Novak. Nadal would hurt his abductor in the Australian Open quarterfinals and lost to Ferrer but came back to successfully defend his French Open title beating Federer 7-5, 7-6(3), 5-7, 6-1. He made the finals of both Wimbledon and the U.S. Open losing to Novak Djokovic in both.

The rivalry extended into the 2012 season with Nadal losing a 5-set thriller in the Australian Open to Djokovic. The Australian Open final with him and Novak was epic and could have gone either way.

Despite not playing great at the spring hard court tournaments, Nadal could reply on the clay court season to bring him back to form, this of course, was where he has always been at his best. Nadal won Monte Carlo by defeating Djokovic easily in the finals. A few weeks later he defeated Djokovic again in Rome.

Going in as the favorite to win his third consecutive French Open and seventh overall, Nadal would not lose a set going into the finals. As expected, top ranked Novak Djokovic was waiting for Nadal in the finals. This would be the fourth-consecutive major final where these two would meet. After losing the previous three match-ups, Nadal finally got his revenge and defeated Novak 6-4, 6-3, 2-6, 7-5 in a match that took two days to complete due to rain.

More Injuries:

Nadal's been in incredible form and was hoping to take that momentum into the rest of the season and try to get is #1 ranking back. Sadly, his plans would be derailed with an upset loss in the

2nd round at Wimbledon to Lukas Rosol. It was one of the biggest upsets ever at Wimbledon. As always, Nadal showed class in defeat and did not make any excuses.

The other big misfortune that fell on Nadal was a knee injury and caused him to miss the rest of the 2012 season and start of the 2013 season. Because he wasn't able to play in the 2012 U.S. Open, nor the 2013 Australian Open, Nadal lost many points and his ranking fell to #4, with four titles, one major, and a 42-6 record.

As in the past, Nadal eased his way back into the tennis season by playing on his favored clay surfaces. The clay court season would be exhilarating. After losing to Djokovic in the Monte Carlo finals, Nadal did not lose another clay court match during

the season, including his 8th French Open crown. Nadal defeated Djokovic in an epic semifinal 6-4, 3-6, 6-1, 6-7(3), 9-7 on the way to this title. It was one of the greatest matches ever at the French Open. It was high level tennis. Nadal would then defeat Ferrer in the finals.

Wimbledon, however, would be a huge disappointment. Nadal unexpectedly lost in the first round to Steve Darcis. Nadal did not let this deter him from finishing the rest of the season strong. He won both Masters 1000 summer hard court tournaments and entered the U.S. Open as the flight favorite to win it all.

At the U.S. Open, Nadal was flawless in his first six matches losing only one set along the way. Once again, he would face Djokovic in the finals. Djokovic had his chances to go up two sets to one. However, Nadal kept fighting and took the third set and ran away in the fourth set to win his second U.S. Open title. He would finish #1 for the year.

The 2014 Season And Beyond:

Nadal would reach the 2014 Australian Open final. His opponent was veteran Stan Wawrinka of Switzerland. This was Wawrinka's first final in a major so Nadal was the heavy favorite. Wawrinka got off to a great start taking the first set. Nadal then injured his back severely in the 2nd set. He was not the same after that. Despite Nadal fighting and taking the 3rd set, Wawrinka won and took home his first major record, denying Nadal the opportunity to win his 14th major title.

Injuries would be a recurring theme for Nadal in 2014. He looked very average on the clay courts going into the French Open- he lost in Monte Carlo and Barcelona. He managed to win in Madrid but was crushed by Djokovic in the finals at Rome.

One would have thought that his record on clay in the 2014 season did not bode well for his French Open chances, but this didn't stop Nadal in the slightest. He played vintage Rafael Nadal tennis during the second week in particular. He won his 9th French Open Championship. It was a truly incredible accomplishment where persistence, desire, and hard work paid off. He further cemented his title as the greatest ever clay court player.

Nadal suffered an injury to his wrist after being eliminated in the 4th round at Wimbledon. Nadal would miss the summer hard courts and the U.S. Open.

The 2015 season was especially rough, Nadal returned nowhere near the level of player he had once been. He was losing to players he had never lost to. He was no longer a top player. Something was missing. The forehands were not as precise, and his confidence was lagging. It appeared that age and injuries had begun to catch up with Nadal. In 2015, he failed to win a major for the first time since 2004.

A first-round loss to Fernando Verdasco in the 2016 Australian Open was indicative of how the rest of his year would go. He was unable to play the last three months of 2016 due to a continued wrist injury.

The 2017 season didn't look any better for Nadal, yet he proved everyone wrong. Nadal added a new coach in Carlos Moya and this seemed to signal a new era in Nadal's game. He returned to the high level of tennis he had previously been at and worked his way into the finals of the Australian Open. His eventual loss to Federer in that final didn't matter because Nadal was on the mend and displaying a renaissance of his old form. Nadal dominated on clay winning three tournaments and finally getting back his French Open crown, his 10th. He was nearly unbeatable on clay that year.

He was striking the ball better than ever and fought his way back to the #1 ranking. In addition, Nadal would win his third U.S. Open title. He was 67-11 with 6 titles, two Masters 1000 titles, and two majors. Nadal would follow up 2018 with his 11th French Open crown- still showing everyone that he has the fight in him to be competitive well over a decade into his storied career.

WHAT WE CAN LEARN FROM RAFAEL NADAL

R afael Nadal has proven to be an outstanding role model both on and off the court. In his style of play, we see someone who strikes the ball with pure intensity and gives his full effort to run down every point like it is his last. The energy he shows is unmatched.

His off-court persona belies the attacking nature of his game. During interviews and press conferences he displays a boyish smile and humble nature. His respect for others including those of his peers and fellow tennis champions is remarkable. Nadal has said it was such an honor to practice with John McEnroe. Of his rival Roger Federer, Nadal says that Federer is the greatest of all-time in the history of the sport.

Rafael Nadal is also an exceptional ambassador of the sport. He understands how impactful his presence is to kids that look up to him and he is always willing to stop for a selfie and autograph. At his academy he's able to teach the younger generation about the physical and mental part of the game.

Find a Mentor:

Having the support of a great family upbringing has undoubt- edly been a large part of who Rafa is today, but it was the special mentoring from one person who may have made the difference between a merely successful tennis career and the stellar run as champion Nadal has experienced. Uncle Toni was the teacher, mentor, and 'rock' Nadal needed. This is the first lesson that we can learn from Rafa's story- find a mentor.

Get a coach, mentor, or an accountability buddy. Having one of these people in your corner is one of the greatest gifts you can give yourself. These are people that care about you and want the best for you. These people will also push you to get your life to the next level. When you have doubts about what you can do, they will not let you off the hook or quit.

As a result of the coaching and mentorship of Uncle Toni, Rafael Nadal was able to push harder and play with more intensity than he otherwise could have.

A great example of Uncle Toni's contribution came prior to the 2009 Australian Open Final. In his biography "Rafa," Nadal mentions the events following an exhausting five set semi-final with Fernando Verdasco. Nadal admitted that his body was stiff, and his legs were heavy; he was lightheaded and dizzy as well. In the book, Nadal recounted that he considered not playing the final and giving Roger Federer the walkover win. In his mind, he conceded the match to Roger.

However, Uncle Toni was not going to have any of it.

Per Rafa's biography Toni said, "Look, when you get on the court I assure you that you won't feel any better. You'll probably feel worse. So, it's up to you whether you rise above the pain and the exhaustion and summon up the desire you need to win."

Rafa replied, "Toni, I'm sorry, I can't see it. I just can't."

Toni said, "Don't say you can't, because anybody who digs deep enough can always find the motivation they need for anything. In war, people do things that appear to be impossible. Just imagine if there were a guy sitting behind you in the stadium pointing a gun at you, telling you that if you didn't run, and keep running, he'd shoot you. I bet you run then, so come on!" Toni also mentioned, "this is your big chance. Bad as you might be feeling now, it's likely that you'll never have as good a chance of winning the Australian Open as you do today. And even if there's only a one percent chance of you winning this match, well then, you have to squeeze every last drop out of that one percent."

As a result, Rafa laced up his shoes for another five-set match. He prevailed in the end defeating Federer to win his first Australian Open title. Motivation like this has no price tag. Imagine having a coach who could get you to perform like this in life.

If you want to take your business to the next level, improve your relationships or health, a good first step would be to find a coach or mentor to help you get to where you want to be.

Practice Patience:

Nadal has said, "…patience is not passive waiting. Patience is active acceptance of the process required to attain your goals and dreams." Now, Rafael Nadal's aggressive style of play does not necessarily evoke an image of patience but if you look closely at how he composes himself you'll see he has this trait in spades.

Nadal has no 'panic button,' zero. He waits for his opportunities. For example, after the first set of the 2006 French Open Final against Roger Federer, where he lost the set 6-1, he kept his composure to come back and win the next three sets. In the 2008 Wimbledon Final he rode out the storm when Roger was looking unstoppable at times. His successes have come from embracing the process when he falls behind.

Another way in which Rafael Nadal has had to practice patience is during the no-less-than 15 times during his career that he has missed action on the court due to injury. His foot, knee, back, wrist, and abdominal muscles have all kept him off the court at one stage or another, but he has come back even stronger every time.

Embracing a mindset of patience and resilience allows us the foresight to wait for our opportunities. In a world where many seek out immediate gratification, focusing on long-term goals and embracing the journey is really the path to our dreams. It takes commitment and time to achieve a desired outcome. As Rafael Nadal states, "...he who has patience and work ethic can always end up with what he will."

Enjoy and Live Out Each Moment in Full:

Tennis fans have witnessed Rafael Nadal play with intensity on every point. He is only focused on the point at hand and takes no points off no matter what the score is. Playing this way frustrates his opponents, especially on clay. This strategy has helped Rafa win 11 French Open titles to date because he takes no points off.

Living for the moment is a practice, but it is extremely rewarding. In my own experience, I have found practicing meditation has lessened my stress and anxiety and ensure I stay in the present as much as I can. Meditation offers one means of staying in the moment. I would also argue that being at practice on in a match is like a meditation practice to Rafa. During many matches, many players have believed they had Rafa beat, only to learn that he would continue to persist.

In the 2013 French Open semifinal against Djokovic was able to break Nadal's serve in the fifth set and only had to hold serve to gain a berth into the finals. However, Nadal refused to relent and played every point one at a time. He waited for his opportunity and broke Djokovic and won the fifth set 9-7. Rafa would go on to defeat David Ferrer in the finals to capture his 8th French Open title.

2008 WIMBLEDON FINAL

By the time he had reached the 2008 Wimbledon Men's Final, Rafael Nadal had already begun cementing a legacy as the 'King of Clay.' He was a four-time winner of the French Open (with many more of those titles to come later) but winning a championship at Wimbledon was his ultimate dream. In 1996 Manuel Santana was the last Spaniard to win it all so this was also a point of pride for Nadal to do it not only for himself but for his country.

Adding to the drama of the moment was that Nadal would be facing Roger Federer, who had already defeated him in previous Wimbledon Finals. Nadal was determined to win the title. He was making his move to number 1 in the rankings. After recently defeating Federer at the French Open Final 6-1, 6-3, 6-0, Nadal won the Queens Club Championships (the tune-up to Wimbledon) which was promising. He came into the final match with a great two weeks of play behind him in the tournament- but Federer was also looking very strong deep into the tournament. There was an incredible amount of excitement and match hype going into the final.

Set 1:

The match started with Federer first to serve. Nadal's form and focus during the first rally of the match were obvious. He was already making Federer move from one side of the court to the other. Right away, Nadal was sending a message that he intended to take control early on. Despite losing the first point, Federer held serve at 1-0 in the first game. Federer was showing no signs of ill-effect after his defeat at the French Open Final. He was playing on his best surface and was clearly locked-in and ready to battle as well.

On his own first service game of the match, Nadal delivered an ace. His service strategy was very clear- put pressure on Federer's backhand. Nadal would go on to hold and bring the score to 1-1.

In the third game, with Federer serving, the match began to open up. Federer came through with a brilliant touch volley. 15-0. Nadal took advantage of a second serve to win the next point. 15-15. Nadal pushed forward to get an early break point and was able to capitalize on the opportunity. Nadal draws first blood by breaking Federer's serve and going up a break in the first set, two games to one. Nadal would then consolidate the break by holding his own serve and going up 3-1 in the first set. Nadal was serving very efficiently, but Federer would come back and easily hold to avoid another break to make it 3-2 Nadal.

The set score would reach 5-4 with Nadal maintaining his lead and he was ready to serve for the first set. He started by getting Federer to produce a backhand return error. 15-0. On the next point, Federer drew even at 15-15 when Nadal made an unforced error. They go back and forth in this manner when the score is finally 40-30 set point for Nadal.

Unsurprisingly, Federer does not let the first set go quietly. He brings the score back to deuce with a great hustle play. Federer then earns a break point on a forehand volley winner. Nadal caught a break when Federer hits a long volley and the score returns to deuce. Nadal then earned another set point by serving his first ace of the match. Federer then hit a beautiful cross-court forehand to force an error on Nadal. By this time Federer had erased two set points and, in the process, earned himself another break point. Nadal countered Federer's momentum by capitalizing on a weak return by Federer on a second serve. As a result, Nadal would earn another set point chance as Federer hit one long and the advantage was back with Nadal. On set point number three, Nadal would not be denied. He won the first set 6-4.

Set 2:

Federer was to serve to start the second set and held easily at love. 1-0 Federer. Nadal's serve started on shaky ground as Federer raced out to a 0-30 lead by playing two brilliant points. Nadal would find his composure and even the score at 30-30 by winning the next two points. But it wasn't enough to hold back Federer who would go on to get a break point and convert it to a 2 games to love lead. The set then quickly became a 3-0 score for Federer because of this momentum. In Nadal's autobiography, he talks about this moment of the match when Federer becomes unstoppable. Nadal indicated that the best and only strategy that worked when Roger was on a roll like this was to 'ride out the storm' and hope that it passes sooner rather than later.

Nadal went back to work and was not discouraged. He managed to bring the score to 3-1, then Federer would hold his own serve again and take a commanding 4-1 lead. Nadal held the next game bringing the score to 4-2.

On the seventh game in the second set at 15-15, Federer missed a volley when Nadal put some pressure on him. Nadal then had a chance to convert on the break to get back on serve and gain back the momentum. After several incredible rallies, Nadal clawed his way back into the set and brought the score to 4-4.

At 4-4 with Federer serving, Nadal showed his tenacity and attacked to gain a lead of 0-30. Only Nadal's persistence was able to keep Federer from running away with the set early on. Nadal had a huge chance to break again after he increased his game lead 0-40. At 15-40, Nadal hit a forehand winner to go up a break. He had won four straight games at this time and with the score at 5-4 in favor of Nadal he was ready to serve out the second set.

Federer won the first point by playing aggressively on the return for an easy forehand volley winner. Nadal's then served up an ace to bring the score to 15-15, followed by a forehand down the line to give him a 30-15 lead. Another volley winner by Federer made the score even at 30-30, and finally, Nadal's slice cross-court backhand gave him a set point. Federer was able to fight back and even the score as well as create a break point opportunity for himself, but alas Nadal remained steady and won the second set 6-4. Nadal now held a huge two sets to love lead.

Despite the score, Federer was playing some great tennis, but it was Nadal who was charging and it was paying off. Nadal did not seem to be letting down in the slightest during those first two sets. It appeared that Nadal was on his way to winning Wimbledon at this point.

Set 3:

At this point, Nadal's relentlessness and persistence had gotten him up two sets to none. If Federer was going to win his 6th Wimbledon, he would have a long, steep mountain to climb. His opening service game in the third set was looking to be his most important service game of the match. Displaying his usual grace under pressure, Federer held easily at love. But Nadal held and kept on serve.

The score at 1-1 in the third set, a scary moment came when

Nadal went down and seemed to hurt his right knee. He immediately dispelled any concerns of injury when he immediately got up and hit a beautiful backhand crosscourt. Nothing was going to keep Nadal down.

After a few games, and with the set score at 3-3 Nadal gave himself a 0-40 triple break point opportunity on Federer's serve. A break at this point of the match would likely have meant Nadal would be ten minutes or so away from victory. But Federer is no ordinary opponent and he managed to escape this predicament with his clutch serving and remain on serve with a set score of 4-3.

Despite the score, this match is being played at a high level by both players.

At 5-5 in the third set, the level of play remains high. Nadal is not discouraged at having lost triple break point at all, and Federer seems unphased that he is two sets down. They go back and forth and eventually are forced into a third set tiebreaker.

With the tiebreaker, Nadal served at 0-1 and quickly equalized to 1-1 on a Federer backhand error. Nadal would then hit a nice one-two combo serve and volley to go up 2-1. Federer, during his service, challenged on a forehand that was called out, but the replay showed it in. Thus, the point was played over. Federer then served up an ace to make it 2-2. He quickly made it 3-2 with another ace.

On Nadal's next serve, he was forced into an error by pressure from Federer's forehand. Federer now had a 4-2 tiebreak lead. Nadal then hit his next serve and Federer hit an inside-out forehand winner to go up 5-2. Nadal did manage to get one point back on Roger's serve, however, Nadal was unable to handle a wide serve delivered by Federer, suddenly Federer was sitting on three set point opportunities.

Nadal continued to fight for the third set and brought the tiebreak score to 6-4 on an overhead winner. Nadal then served an ace to cut down Federer's lead to 6-5. On the next point, Federer served up an ace, when up 7-5, and took the third set.

Set 4:

With brilliant play by both players, it only seemed appropriate for this match to extend to at least a fourth set. Federer served brilliantly and held his nerve to get to the fourth set. Nadal's tenacious play required Roger to hit an extra ball each time.

Nadal served first in the fourth set with a routine hold. Federer would counter in the next game with brilliant shot-making to even the fourth set at 1-1.

Both players went back and forth, held serve, showed their extremely powerful forehands- they are fighting for every point.

At 5-6 they still remained on serve and Federer was tasked with serving for the tiebreak. Nadal came out firing and got the first point but Federer held and brought the fourth set to another tiebreaker.

Nadal served to start the fourth set tiebreaker. Right away a brilliant exchange occurred. Nadal appeared to win the point with a beautiful backhand overhead, but it went to Federer's forehand and he countered with a down the line winner, 1-0 Federer. Nadal then hit a forehand winner to make it 1-1. A wide forehand shot by Federer then gave Nadal a 2-1 lead and mini break. Nadal then stretched the lead 3-1 on an ace wide to Federer's backhand. The score quickly went to 4-1 to Nadal with a serve that kicked back on the line, forcing Federer to hit it into the net. Federer got a point back on his next serve to make it 4-2 Nadal as the players switch ends.

Then at 4-2, Federer hit a wide forehand to make it 5-2 and Nadal had the opportunity to put away the match on his next two serves.

At 5-2, Nadal uncharacteristically double-faulted and brought the score to 5-3. It was the first time that nerves seemed to interfere with Nadal's play. Federer once again prevailed on the next point to make it 5-4 and then quickly tied it, 5-5. Federer is showed tremendous courage in the fight back and puts himself in position at 6-5 to steal the tiebreak and fourth set.

In another great rally, Roger hit a wide forehand and the score became 6-6. The players switched ends again.

Nadal earned his first championship point opportunity when Federer hit a forehand just long. Federer challenged the call, but it was confirmed out. Federer served at 6-7 and hit a solid first serve to tie it at 7 all.

On the next point, Federer appeared to have hit a winner down the line, but Nadal answered with authority on an incredible running forehand that just got past Roger for the winner, 8-7 Nadal. It was the shot of the match and gave Nadal Championship point #2. This time Nadal gets to serve for the championship.

Nadal served to Federer's backhand and Federer blocked it with a defensive return. Nadal then hit his bread and butter topspin forehand to the Federer backhand, and Federer hit a backhand beautifully down the line for a winner. Two of the greatest shots in this match occurred back-to-back by both players. The tiebreak score was now at 8-8.

With Nadal still serving, another great exchange led to a Federer winner and another set point. At 9-8, and Federer prepared to serve and to take the match to a fifth set.

Federer served, and Nadal hit a backhand return long, fourth set Federer 7-6 (8). At this point, the crowd was going wild at witnessing such an unbelievably competitive match. The team boxes of both players were on their feet each time their player won a point. Nadal's father was visibly anxious, as was the Federer camp. Yet, both teams showed excitement and support. It was only fitting that this match would go to a fifth set between these two epic warriors.

At this point, Nadal would have been feeling frustrated having been up 5-2 in the tiebreak with two championship point opportunities. The challenge for Nadal was keeping the intensity and fighting on after the disappointment of lost chances.

Set 5:

With the rain delays, Wimbledon was getting dark. The fifth set started at 7:30 pm London time. Federer served first and held. Nadal overcame the nerves of the last set and held to make it 1-1.

Nadal made the third game competitive and forced it to deuce by capitalizing on errors by Federer, whose level of play had dropped ever-so-slightly after an emotional fourth set win. Nadal persisted in getting a second deuce, but Federer managed to still hold to make it 2-1.

Nadal then held to make it 2-2. At this time, there was another rain delay. People began to speculate whether the match would be able to continue or would need to carry to the next day.

Fortunately, it was not a long delay and at 2-2 with the game score at deuce, Federer won the next two points with two aces, 3-2 in the fifth set.

At 2-3, Nadal opened up his serve with a forehand passing shot by Federer. Nadal's mental toughness was apparent. He ended up holding and it was 3-3. Federer made easy work of his next service game and held at love to make it 4-3.

At 30-30, Federer hit his best forehand down the line to earn the first break point chance in the fifth set. Nadal fought it off with an easy overhead winner. At deuce, Nadal hit a strong second serve and won the rally to get the advantage and he pulled out the game, 4-4.

Federer then held to bring the score to 5-4. Nadal remained in the moment and hit a clever second serve to go up 15-0. Federer got it back to 30-30, but Nadal used strong first serves in on the next two points to push through and win the game, and leveled the fifth set score at 5-5.

The next game, Nadal earned a double break point chance with a forehand winner, but Federer then served an ace and won the point to get it to deuce. Federer managed to win the next two points to hold again, 6-5 Federer.

Nadal held again to make it 6-6. Being the fifth set, there would be no tiebreak. Federer and Nadal were forced to continue going head to head.

Nadal got out to a 0-30 lead in the thirteenth game. Federer got it back to 30-30 and then to 40-30 on a strong first serve. Federer missed a wide-open volley and it was back at deuce. Eventually, Federer was able to win that game, but it seemed Nadal's tenacious and persistent play was beginning to wear down Federer.

At 7-6 Federer had the lead and Nadal was getting ready to serve to stay in the match. Federer drew first blood to make it 0-15. He hit the next shot long to even the score at 15-15. Nadal forced a score of 30-15 with a great body serve. Nadal then won the next point on a winner, 40-15. A bad bounce on the net favored Federer, 40-30. On the next point, Nadal displayed tremendous movement and athleticism with a forehand winner. Federer played great defense, but it was such an outstanding point by Nadal covering the court beautifully, 7-7, fifth set.

With Federer serving, Nadal got the point on a forehand winner, 0-15. Federer then made an unforced error to make it 0-30. Federer managed to make it 15-30 on a forehand winner. Nadal then returned the favor with a tremendous backhand crosscourt winner from behind the baseline. With double break point on the line, Federer served a clutch ace to make it 30-40. The score then reached deuce when Nadal miss-hit a ball going long, deuce. Nadal then got another break point when Federer hit a forehand long. Once again, Federer came up with a first serve ace, deuce. Nadal kept the pressure on when Federer hit one in the net. Nadal had yet another break point chance.

Federer then hit a forehand that went slightly long and Nadal finally broke Federer's serve for the first time since it was 4-4 in the second set, 8-7 Nadal.

This was another high-pressure moment of the match. Nadal had a few championship point opportunities in the fourth set tiebreaker. He was sitting on another a chance to serve for the championship.

After such furious play by both sides, by the time Nadal's critical service starts the clock is already at 9 pm London time and it is getting dark. The fans with their cell phones provided the needed light to the players. It was unimaginable, yet, if Roger broke back, there would be a chance the match could be suspended until the next day. Everyone involved was hoping a winner would be crowned on this day.

The first point Nadal hit was long, and Federer took a 0-15 lead. Once again, Nadal's serve got him out of trouble with a serve and volley winner, 15-15. An easy put away made it 30-15 for Nadal. Federer got it back to 30-30 when Nadal hit the ball that could have gone long by Federer, but he flicked it back and went long. It was 40-30 and another championship point for Nadal when Federer's backhand went wide. Federer once again denied Nadal with a beautiful backhand return error, deuce. Nadal came up with a great serve wide to Federer's forehand that Federer misses, advantage Nadal and Championship point again.

Nadal stepped up to serve and he hit it again to Federer's forehand. Federer got it back to Nadal, and Nadal hit a backhand to Federer's forehand. Federer's forehand though sailed into the net, and with that point a Rafael Nadal wins his first Wimbledon

Championship.

The final score was 6-4, 6-4, 6-7(5), 6-7(7), 9-7. It was a truly special and spectacular match with many people including commentator John McEnroe believing it may have been the greatest match ever played.

There was a very warm handshake exchange between Nadal and Federer. Both had their arms around each other. Nadal's team was elated. Federer's father stood up and clapped, showing tremendous class in defeat. The entire Federer camp was dignified during such a defeat. Federer's then girlfriend, now wife, Mirka congratulated Nadal as he went to the stands to his team to embrace them. It was a beautiful moment for the new Wimbledon Champion.

Both players gave us something very special, and we will be talking about this match 50 years from now. Both played like champions and gave a tremendous effort. As far as Rafael Nadal, it gave him his Wimbledon. Nadal served incredibly, only being broken once. This match could easily be called the greatest match of his career, even over his 10th French Open title.

This win at Wimbledon proved he was more than just a great clay court player. Nadal's hard work, desire, commitment, and dedication to improving his game on all surfaces paid off. Wimbledon was always Nadal's dream, and he accomplished it. Within a month, Nadal became the #1 men's tennis player in the world for the first time ever. It was the first time someone other than Roger Federer was number once since January 2004. Nadal would also finish #1 for the year.

CONSISTENCY
ROGER FEDERER

CONSISTENCY

"You have to believe the long-term plan you have, but you need the short-term goals to motivate and inspire you."

"Once you find that peace, that place of peace and quiet, harmony and confidence, that's when you start playing your best"

- Roger Federer

C onsistency is the main feature that defines Roger Federer's incredible tennis career. In 15 years from 2003 to 2017, he has defined this modern era of tennis. Federer was the first of the Big Four to break through and establish himself as a legend. He is one of the most beloved tennis champions ever as well as one of the most recognizable athletes in the world. Federer's fan base around the world is wide-ranging and diverse.

At 6'1" and 187 pounds, Federer has the ideal physique of a tennis player. His stature mixed with an incredible all-around game is a breathtaking combination to watch. His game is beautiful to watch for its completeness and harkens to the old school finesse of eras past. The serve and volley game that Federer developed is a clear nod to his idols Boris Becker, Stefan Edberg, and Pete Sampras.

Yet, Federer is still a decidedly modern champion. He had to adjust the traditional serve and volley game due to the changing of the racquet and string technology. Federer adapted by developing a strong baseline game and playing in an offensive style by striking the ball early. As a result, Federer grew to have an incredible all-around game. His movement is silky, smooth, effortless, and graceful. He is known as the maestro and moves on the court as Mikhail Baryshnikov does on the stage.

Picking apart the different elements of his overall game provides an even more remarkable portrait of tennis greatness. Roger Federer might be the best shot maker tennis has ever seen. He is known for his powerful forehand that he controls and finesses to whichever angle suits the situation. If an opponent hits a short ball to Federer's forehand, point over. Federer's serve is among the best in today's game because of the variety. He places the serve beautifully and can kick the serve as well. As for his backhand, Federer has great slice and variety. Interestingly, prior to 2017, Federer's backhand did not have power and was considered his only Achilles heel. Yet, he was able to develop a powerful backhand when he came back from injury in 2017 and won the Australian Open, Wimbledon, and 2018 Australian Open. The willingness to improve what is already a near perfect game is a hallmark of Federer's longevity.

He has dominated the men's game for many years and is about to complete his 21st year on the tour. With 20 major titles and closing in 100 titles for his career, Roger's consistency on the tour has been incredible. This is a remarkable outcome considering how inconsistent his results were in his early years on the pro tour when he was trying to break through to the top of the rankings.

Early Life:

Roger Federer was born on August 8, 1981, in Basel, Switzerland to Robert Federer and Lynette Durand. He has one older sister, Diana. Roger's mother is South African and as a result, he holds dual citizenship in Switzerland and South Africa. Unlike Andy Murray, Novak Djokovic, and Rafael Nadal, Federer was not born into an athletic family.

He first picked up a racquet around the age of 4. His love of tennis began when he watched Boris Becker win Wimbledon in 1985. Even though the Federer family did not have an athletic background, they loved tennis. Young Roger did show great ability as an athlete playing basketball, soccer, badminton, and of course tennis. Eventually, he chose to commit to tennis and became one of the top junior players in Switzerland.

Some recognized Roger's talents around this time. However, Roger had one weakness, his temper. Roger would throw his racquet and lose his temper quite frequently. Roger's parents were mortified when they saw his behavior on the court.

At age 10, Roger got a coach named Peter Carter. Carter was a tough and hard-working tennis player who won the men's doubles title with Darren Cahill at the 1985 Australian Open. Carter was able to work with Roger on his game and temperament. He effectively conveyed to Roger how much energy was being wasted on outbursts. Along with teaching the mental side of the game, Carter taught Roger to be gracious and polite, whether he won or lost.

Roger's life was tennis. He spent more time with Peter Carter than his family. Roger would train at Switzerland's National Training Center with a rigorous schedule that only included trips home on the weekends. By the time he reached 16 years of age, Roger's game was beginning to mature and his natural talent was beginning to evolve. Peter Lundgren joined Peter Carter to coach Roger and made a formidable team. In 1998, the hard work that he had been putting in was translating into hardware. Roger became the boy's singles champion at Wimbledon and was a finalist at the U.S. Open- losing to future rival David Nalbandian. Roger also turned pro in 1998.

A Shaky Start:

For someone who has been exceptionally consistent throughout his career, Federer's start on the pro tour was anything but consistent. Around 1999, Peter Lundgren became Roger's full-time coach. Peter Carter remained as a consultant and friend to Roger, someone he could ask advice from every now and then, but for the most part, Carter was no longer a part of the day-to-day team.

Following success in the juniors, Federer began to gradually gain recognition with his match results, including the finals in his hometown in Basel. There were concerns from experts whether he had the hunger and meanness to be a great champion. Some wondered whether Federer would be like Marcelo Rios who had incredible God-given talent but could not channel it, especially on the mental side.

Federer, however, was progressing nicely in his development. In 2001, at the age of 19, he won his first ATP title in Milan, Italy. He followed that feat by single-handedly taking out the United States in the first round of the Davis Cup. Federer defeated Todd Martin on the first day. The second day, he teamed with Lorenzo Mahta to defeat Justin Gimblestob and Jan-Michael Gambill in doubles. Federer then clinched the win for Switzerland defeating Jan-Michael Gambill in singles on the third and final day.

Facing Greatness:

In the 2001 Wimbledon tournament, Federer progressed well and looked to be a natural grass court player- reminiscent of past greats who had dominated on the surface. In the fourth round, when the draw pitted Federer against Wimbledon legend Pete Sampras, there was excitement to see how Federer would stack up. But no-one could anticipate how significant this match would be for Federer against the seven-time champion.

Federer had modeled his game like Sampras in many ways with great service placement, breathtaking volleys, and a powerful forehand. Sampras was struggling in 2001 and past his prime but he was still a standout on the tour. Both players showed up with their best on that day and were handily exchanging points back and forth. The thing to remember about Sampras was even if he was not performing well in the year, he always seemed to find his game at Wimbledon and this year was no different. Yet, Federer did not back down from his idol.

The first set went to a tiebreaker with Federer prevailing on the 16th point. Sampras fought back to take the second set 7-5. They split the next two sets to force a fifth and deciding set. With no fifth set tiebreaker, Sampras was serving 5-6 down on a double break. He hit a solid first serve, but it is to Federer's strike zone on the forehand side. Federer smashed it for the winner. He defeated Sampras in their only professional meeting 7-6(7), 5-7, 6-4, 6-7(2), 7-5. In this moment, the long-reigning king of Wimbledon was dethroned. And appropriately, the man who dealt the blow would be on the verge of beginning his own dynasty. It was a bittersweet moment for Federer because it would be the only time that he faced Sampras on the tour. Federer was also conflicted knowing that he had defeated one of his idols and had a hand in ending what was an incredible run.

Federer's win at Wimbledon against Sampras was professionally very significant, but he would have to wait longer before he could call himself champion. After his glorious fourth-round performance, he would lose to Britain's Tim Henman in the quarters.

Tragedy and Perspective:

The remainder of Federer's 2001 results was inconsistent. He made another finals appearance in Basel, losing to Henman. He had a few early round exits as well. However, with fellow peer, Lleyton Hewitt finishing 2001 with the number one ranking, it appeared only a matter of time that Federer would also elevate to the top of the game.

The following year would be pivotal in Roger Federer's development. The year 2002 began where the previous year left off, with a string of performances on the court that was up and down. He did win three titles, including his first Masters 1000 on the clay in Hamburg, Germany over Marat Safin. Yet, Roland Garros and Wimbledon resulted in first round exits and he also lost first round matches in Canada and Cincinnati. Coming into a tournament it was very difficult to predict which Roger would show up.

This is the same year that tragedy struck Team Federer, personally and professionally. While Roger was in Toronto, Canada for the Masters 1000, former coach and still-close friend Peter Carter died. Peter was tragically killed in a car accident in South Africa while on a safari vacation.

Roger was completely devastated by the news. Carter had been the most important coach Roger had and was like a family member of the Federers. Roger headed back to Basel, Switzerland to attend his friend's funeral right after Cincinnati. For Roger, he recounts how losing a friend changed his perspective about his game. He realized how unimportant tennis was. According to Rene Stauffer in his book, The Roger Federer Story Roger stated, "Any defeat in tennis is nothing compared to such a moment."

This event changed Federer. It was a tragedy that forced him to reevaluate how he saw life and tennis. He learned that tomorrow is not guaranteed, and life is a gift.

From then on, Federer stopped looking at his slump in 2002 in a negative light. Instead of being a victim, he decided to honor Peter Carter on and off the tennis court. Federer decided to apply all of Peter's teachings. He behaved on the court showing grace and sportsmanship, win or lose. Federer has gone on to become a multiple winner of the ATP Sportsmanship Award.

Once Federer returned to the tour after Peter Carter's funeral, his performance progressed and improved, he won in Vienna and qualified for his first ATP Finals. Federer also made it past the round robin into the semifinals losing a hard-fought battle to top-ranked Lleyton Hewitt.

Roger Federer dedicated his success to Peter Carter because Peter's death gave Roger perspective and erased all his doubts in his abilities.

ROGER'S CONSISTENCY YEAR IN AND YEAR OUT

The Breakthrough

A s 2003 approached, there was optimism that Federer would build on the momentum from the 2002 ATP Finals. At the Australian Open, he lost in the round of 16 to David Nalbandian but followed with victories in both Marseille and Dubai.

However, Federer's showing in the French Open was less-than-impressive. He lost in the first round in three sets. This loss was Federer's biggest wakeup call. He has said that this was the single match that motivated and pushed him to get beyond just being a player with great potential and no results.

He would turn his attention to Wimbledon.

Federer played the Wimbledon tune-up in Halle, Germany and won. This was a confidence boost to Federer, especially important because he wanted to avoid the disastrous result of the previous year when he was eliminated in the first round.

Roger Federer had an excellent showing in the first week and went through his matches without losing a single set. got. On the way, he defeated Feliciano Lopez and Sjeng Schalken to reach his first semifinals at Wimbledon. His opponent would be the up-and-coming talent Andy Roddick. This match was deemed as a meeting of two future rivals and champions. Roddick had his chances in the first set, but Federer prevailed in a close tiebreaker and won the next two sets to make the finals.

Waiting for Federer in the finals was a hard-serving Mark Philippoussis from Australia. Federer held his nerve and outplayed Philippoussis despite being forced into two tiebreakers. Federer had finally reached his potential and won his first major title. He won what would be the first of many Wimbledon trophies. Federer was naturally emotional during the trophy ceremony as he joined his idols of Sampras, Becker, and Edberg as a Wimbledon Champion.

Roger Federer was on track to achieving greatness, and his future looked incredibly bright. By the end of 2003 he had rounded out the year with his first ATP Finals Championship by defeating legend Andre Agassi, he earned a record of 78 wins and 17 losses and captured 7 titles.

Becoming #1:

Federer started 2004 strong with an impressive showing at the Australian Open tournament. He defeated former #1 player Lleyton Hewitt in the round of 16, David Nalbandian in the quarters, and disposed of 2003 French Open Champion Juan Carlos Ferrero during the semis.

The finals would be a match-up with another player slated to be one of the next greats, Russia's Marat Safin. Like Federer, Safin was an incredibly gifted tennis player. Federer would defeat Safin that night and capture his second major and first Australian Open title. This would also mark the beginning of Roger Federer's #1 ranking, a streak that would last for an impressive

237 weeks.

Federer continued the momentum of his Australian Open win by winning in Dubai and capturing his first Indian Wells title. His streak came to an end in Miami when he lost in the second round to an unknown Rafael Nadal. At the time, there was little indication of how both players would elevate tennis and fan interest to new heights. It would be the beginning of a special rivalry.

Turning Potential Into Success:

During the 2004 Wimbledon Championships that summer, Federer would not lose a set heading into the quarterfinals. Awaiting was Lleyton Hewitt, whom Federer defeated in four sets. After another victory in the semifinals against Sebastian Grosjean from France, Federer would meet Andy Roddick in the finals.

Roddick came in with a game plan against Federer, to play aggressively from the baseline. Roddick's plan appeared to be working and he won the first set 6-4. Then a rain delay changed the momentum as Federer fought hard to win the second set, 7-5. The third set was as highly contested, and Federer needed a tiebreaker to put it away, then wrapped it up in the fourth set 6-4. Roger Federer was Wimbledon Champion once again, winning his second title there and his third major overall.

Having strung together wins at recent majors, the inevitable question heading into the U.S. Open was whether Federer could win in New York- a far larger and rowdier stage. Aside from Ivan Lendl and a few others, Europeans have not had much success in New York. New York has traditionally been made up of loud, knowledgeable fans. It wasn't an obvious match for Roger Federer's calm demeanor. What Federer did have going for him was a hardcourt title win over Andy Roddick in Toronto prior to the U.S. Open. Federer was playing incredible tennis.

Federer got off to a strong start only having lost one set in the first three rounds. He was handed a walkover in the fourth round when Andrei Pavel withdrew. This set up a showdown again two-time U.S. Open Champion and fan favorite Andre Agassi. This was the ultimate New York test for Federer who was not quite the adoring fan favorite yet. Virtually the entire crowd was behind Agassi. Age and injuries were catching up to the American, however Agassi was rounding into form playing excellent tennis as well.

Federer got off to the good start he needed and captured the first set, 6-3. Agassi battled back and took the second set, 6-2. Federer then won a hard fought third set, 7-5. Amid this excitement the rains then came, and the match was suspended to the next afternoon.

The next day, Agassi would take the fourth set 6-3 to force a decisive fifth set in extremely windy conditions. Federer prevailed in the fifth set and was elated. He understood how massive a step it was beat a great American tennis player on his home soil.

In the semifinals Federer beat Tim Henman of Great Britain to set up the final against 2001 U.S. Open Champion, Lleyton Hewitt. For quite some time, Hewitt had the upper hand on Federer, but Federer had a clear advantage in this matchup having beat Hewitt recently in the 2004 Australian Open and Wimbledon. This meeting was no different. With Federer playing nearly perfect tennis early in the match, he beat Hewitt in 3 sets, 6-0, 7-6, 6-0. Federer claimed his first U.S. Open. He also became the first player to win three majors in one year since Mats Wilander in 1988.

Roger Federer finished 2004 with a dominant 74-6 win-loss record with 11 titles and his first #1 finish. He was no longer the player with great potential. He was living it.

Going from Strength To Strength:

When it looked as though he could not have a better year than the one had he posted in 2004, Roger Federer became even more of a force in 2005.

He was, of course, the fan favorite to defend his Australian Open crown. Going into the semifinals, Federer had not lost a set. His match against Marat Safin in the semifinals, however, was an absolute battle of two enormously talented players. Safin would prevail in the fifth set winning 9-7 and dethroning Roger. It was one of the Australian Open's greatest matches. Federer had his opportunities, but it was Safin's day.

Despite the letdown at the first major of the year, Federer came back and did not lose a hardcourt match for the remainder of the year. He won titles in Rotterdam and Dubai, Indian Wells, and Miami Open after coming back from two sets down in the finals to Rafael Nadal. On clay Federer captured the title in Hamburg and got to the quarterfinals in Monte Carlo.

On the back of such a positive clay court season, Federer had an opportunity to capture his first French Open and a career slam. He was competitive in the tournament, not dropping a set into the semifinals, but eventually fell short to powerhouse Rafael Nadal.

The 2005 Wimbledon saw challenging draw for Federer as he would face three former #1 players. He would prevail winning his third consecutive Wimbledon title easily defeating Andy Roddick. He also successfully defended his U.S. Open title this year. It would be Federer's 6th major title which would time him with his idols Stefan Edberg and Boris Becker. By the end of the 2005 season Roger Federer finished with a remarkable 81-4 record with 11 titles and two majors. It was one of the greatest seasons a tennis player has ever had.

If 2005 was a great year, 2006 was Federer's masterpiece. He would win three majors in a calendar year once again. For the third consecutive year Roger Federer would dominate the men's tour and reach new heights. His 2006 results stacked up to 92 wins, 5 losses, 3 majors, 4 Masters 1000 titles, and 12 titles overall. The year Federer would have in 2007 would have been a stellar year for any other player but for him at this point in his career 3 majors in one year was almost expected, he was so completely head-and-shoulders above every other competitor during those years. The only hiccup in his game was the clay court but this was more a product of the unique hold Rafa had on the French Open (in which Federer was also a finalist in 2007.)

Roger Federer consistently dominated between 2004 to 2007. However, the year 2008 would be a time of transition for Roger.

Fierce Competition:

In the years immediately preceding 2008, Roger Federer was the one to beat on the ATP tour. Whether his play began to falter, or others began to catch up to his level, more competition began to appear. This was apparent at the beginning of the year in the Australian Open where he was the favorite to defend his Championship

As two-time defending Australian Open Champion, Federer was the favorite to capture his third straight title. In the third round, he battled against Serbia's Janko Tipsarevic. Roger got down two sets to one but eventually escaped with a five-set victory, 6-7(5), 7-6(1), 5-7, 6-1, 10-8. Federer would then defeat Tomas Berdych in the fourth round and James Blake in the quarterfinals. Although he made it through to the tournament, he was not looking sharp.

Awaiting Federer in the semis was Novak Djokovic. Djokovic and Federer had extremely competitive head-to-head play in their two previous matches, and Djokovic was playing with confidence. Despite Federer's 5-2 lead in the first set, Djokovic took the next five games and won the first set. Federer looked flat in the second set losing 6-3 and fought in the third but Djokovic won the tiebreak and earned a spot in the final. This was Federer's first loss in a major outside of the French Open in three years. It also ended Federer's streak of ten consecutive major finals appearances. A small controversy was brewing in Djokovic's box, where chants of the "king is dead" were directed at Federer.

This was the beginning of a series of surprising losses for Federer. He lost in the opening match in Dubai against Britain's Andy Murray, who at the time was another up-and-coming star.

Heading into Indian Wells, news broke that Federer was diagnosed with mononucleosis, the symptoms of which likely affected his 2008 performance thus far. But he did not take time off and played through it. At the tournament, Federer lost in the semifinals to American Mardy Fish for the first time, 6-3, 6-2. It was a very one-sided victory for the 98th ranked Fish. He continued to show mixed results into the clay court season.

Fortunately, he was beginning to find some form again by the time the French Open came around. He was not quite at 100% but was playing well enough to reach his 16th consecutive major semifinal. Federer's consistency was helping him to remain competitive despite his health setbacks. He reached the finals once again to set up another showdown with Rafael Nadal. The highly anticipated final turned into the most lopsided loss Roger Federer had ever had in a major final. Nadal never gave Federer a chance to get in the match and ran away with it 6-1, 6-3, 6-0.

With Wimbledon around the corner, Federer was able to collect a tournament win in the lead up tournament in Halle, Germany. He would be back at Wimbledon attempting to win his sixth straight title.

During the first week, Federer started to look like he was in vintage form. Former #1 Lleyton Hewitt was awaiting him in the fourth round and Federer won in straight sets. Straight set victories followed in the quarters over Mario Ancic of Croatia and in the semis over Marat Safin. The final would be another showdown between Roger Federer and Rafael Nadal. As highlighted in the previous section, the match would be one of the greatest ever played. Nadal prevailed 6-4, 6-4, 6-7(5), 6-7(8), 9-7. Federer would not only lose the title he would lose his #1 ranking that he had held over the previous 4 years to Nadal.

Although reeling from the loss in the Wimbledon final, Federer had a positive Olympics, where he won the gold medal in men's doubles with Stan Wawrinka. This achievement provided some momentum going into the U.S. Open. He was in the unusual position of having not won a major yet that year and only had one more opportunity. Going into the U.S. Open, Nadal was the favorite to win his third major title for the year. Andy Murray had drastically improved his game throughout the year, especially in the summer. AT the opening ceremony, Federer received a warm standing ovation from the fans. He had become loved and adored in New York.

Federer sailed through the first three rounds rather routinely. The fourth round was a battle against Russia's Igor Andreev. Roger found another gear in the fifth set and prevailed 6-7(5), 7-6(5),6-3, 3-6, 6-3.

He once again made the finals to play the first-time finalist Andy Murray. Andy upset an exhausted Nadal in the semis. Despite a winning record against Federer, Murray was overmatched. Federer took, the match right to Murray, and never let him into the match with a 6-2, 7-5, 6-2 win. Much to the relief to himself and his fans, Federer was back to winning majors in time to collect his fifth consecutive U.S. Open title.

Roger Federer's results for 2008 were 66 wins and 15 losses with four titles and one major title. Roger would finish #2, failing to be #1 ranked player since 2003.

A Career Slam:

The goal for 2009 was to get his Wimbledon title back as well as the #1 ranking. Going into the Australian Open, Roger Federer was healthy once again unlike the previous year. The Australian Open would see Federer play some brilliant tennis as well as some battles. One battle would be with Tomas Berdych, which roger would win in five sets. In the semis, Federer defeated Roddick in three sets. His finals opponent would be none other than the #1 ranked player Rafael Nadal.

Federer's semifinal win was routine, but Nadal played a grueling five set match before prevailing against fellow countryman, Fernando Verdasco. Many believed Federer would have the edge since Nadal had the tougher of the two matches and a shorter rest period. It was also their first meeting since the memorable Wimbledon final.

Nadal got off to a fast start winning the first set 7-5. Federer would win the second set 6-3 only to see Nadal take the third set in a tiebreaker. Despite winning the fourth set 6-3, it was Roger Federer who ran out of gas mentally as Nadal ran away in the fifth set 6-2. It would be Nadal's first hardcourt major title. The award ceremony was very emotional as Federer broke down in tears and Nadal consoled him.

The sunshine double in Indian Wells and Miami resulted in two semifinal losses to Murray and Djokovic respectively. Federer played very poorly in the Miami semifinals resulting in him uncharacteristically smashing his racquet. The clay court season resulted in a loss to fellow Swiss Stan Wawrinka in Monte Carlo and another semifinal loss to Novak in Rome. The third clay Masters 1000 was switched from Hamburg to Madrid. Roger Federer would win his first Masters 1000 title in almost two years defeating Nadal in two sets, giving Federer confidence heading into Paris.

The 2009 French Open would be something to remember for Roger Federer and tennis fans. With Nadal ousted in the fourth round to Sweden's Robin Soderling, all eyes were on Federer. The road to the finals wasn't all smooth sailing, but he eventually got there to meet Soderling. The fans were behind Federer, wanting him to complete the career slam and 14th overall major.

Federer broke Soderling right away and played a near perfect first set with tremendous urgency winning 6-1. The second set saw Soderling settle down and be more competitive, however, Federer was nearly flawless in the tiebreaker taking it 7-1. In the third set Federer got the needed break of serve and found himself serving for the championship at 5-4. After a couple of nervous points, Roger Federer had championship point. When Soderling's return sailed into the net, Federer dropped to his knees in absolute joy. He had become the 2009 French Open Champion, 6-1, 7-6(1), 6-4. He would complete the career slam in dramatic fashion. In addition, Roger would tie Pete Sampras for the all-time lead in majors with 14. It would be one of the most memorable moments in Federer's career.

Major History:

Next, Wimbledon was around the corner and would give Federer the opportunity to break the majors record. With Nadal pulling out due to injury, he would not be able to defend his Wimbledon title. Once again, Federer played some great tennis against excellent grass court players. He would beat fellow French finalist Soderling in the fourth round and power server Ivo Karlovic of Croatia in the quarters. Tommy Haas was the opponent in the semis and Federer needed just three sets to put this match away. Federer earned his 7th consecutive Wimbledon

Final appearance.

Roger Federer would play 2004 and 2005 Wimbledon finalist Andy Roddick in a phenomenal match. Roddick was having his best Wimbledon in 2009. He was determined to win his first Wimbledon title and his 2nd major.

The first set was incredibly tight, with Roddick and Federer appearing to be headed into a first set tiebreaker. However, Federer played a loose service game, and Roddick won the first set 7-5. It was Andy Roddick's best set he played against Roger since the 2004 Wimbledon.

In the second set, both players were serving impeccably. Roddick had every opportunity to go up two sets but got a little tight on some points. Federer would fight off four set points (down 6-2) to finally win the tiebreak 8-6. Federer would win another tight tiebreaker 7-5 in the third set to go up two sets to one. Up until this point, Federer had yet to break Roddick's powerful serve. He would not have to if he could hold in the fourth set and win another tiebreaker. However, that plan went out the window.

Roddick broke Federer in the fourth set and went on to win it 6-3. Federer now had to break Roddick at least once if he was going to win his 15th major of all time.

Federer was to serve first, and he held. Roddick of course was still serving bombs. The nail-biting set continued to the thirtieth game of the set. It was 14-15 on serve with Roddick serving. Federer earned a 0-30 lead. Roddick's serve got it back to 30-30 and he had a game point at 40-30. Federer got it back to deuce as Roddick was starting to get fatigued. Roddick got another game point, but Federer got it back to deuce. After an unforced error by Roddick, Federer had a championship point. Roddick would then hit an unforced error into the air and Federer was once gain Wimbledon champion, his sixth Wimbledon in 7 years. The final score was 5-7, 7-6(6), 7-6(5), 3-6, 16-14.

With this win, Roger Federer not only regained his #1 ranking, but he passed Pete Sampras for most majors with 15 titles. It was an incredible accomplishment to achieve. Pete Sampras, along with Rod Laver and Bjorn Borg, were at Centre Court to watch and congratulate Federer.

A Changing Of The Guard:

Not only was the year 2010 the beginning of a new decade, it would also mark the second half of Roger Federer's career. By now, he was already an elder statesman of the game. It started off great as Federer recaptured the Australian Open after a two-year absence- his fourth title Down Under. With this he solidified his #1 ranking and won his 16th major title.

Unfortunately, his form was not great at Indian Wells nor Miami. Going into the clay court season, Federer was hoping to improve. After losing the first round in Rome, Federer played a small clay court tournament in Estoril, Portugal getting into the semifinals before bowing out. He then went to Madrid for his title defense and got to the finals but eventually succumbed to Rafael Nadal.

The next tournament was Federer's title defense at the French Open. Nadal was back and although he hadn't won last year, he was the favorite to recapture the title. Federer was playing well enough to get through the first four rounds but not well enough to beat Robin Soderling in the quarterfinals- a rematch of the previous year's final. It would be the first time Roger would not be in the finals in Roland Garros after 4 consecutive years. It would also end Roger's streak of 23 consecutive semifinals appearance going back six years to the 2004 French Open.

Despite his poor showing at Roland Garros, Wimbledon always presented an opportunity for Roger Federer to reset. It was always the place Federer played his best tennis. In an unlikely turn of events Federer almost lost in the first round after finding himself down two sets to love. He had to fight back and finally was able to pull the match out against Alejandro Falla of Colombia. This was a preview of the troubles that he would experience throughout the tournament this year.

Federer had not found his form going into the quarter finals against Tomas Berdych. Berdych was having a great tournament and dethroned Roger at Wimbledon. After seven consecutive Wimbledon Finals, Federer was out. After the match, Federer admitted to having back problems for much of 2010 and was having quite a deal of pain at Wimbledon. He took some time to rest and recover to get ready for the last leg of the year.

The rest did him well, he made an appearance at the finals in Toronto (losing to Murray) and then won in Cincinnati. It was his first title since winning in Australia earlier in the year. After a successful summer hardcourt series, Federer was poised to get back the trophy at the U.S. Open. But it wasn't to be, he was pitted against perennial rival Novak Djokovic. Although Federer had won in their previous two semi-finals matchups, it was Djokovic who prevailed. This would also mark a changing of the guard for Roger Federer and Novak Djokovic. Djokovic's career would take-off and he would become the dominant player for the next many years. For Roger Federer, the next chapter would be a time of adapting.

Highs And Lows:

The 2011 season would be a year of highs and lows and somewhat of a transition for Federer. His days of single-handedly dominating the tour were over. Roger would turn 30 late in the summer of 2011 and the other three of the big four (Nadal, Djokovic, and Murray) were entering their prime. It would be the first time in eight years that Federer was not the titleholder to any of the four majors. He lost is #2 ranking and slipped to the third spot behind Nadal and Djokovic.

One of the more significant matches of the year for Federer happened at the U.S. Open. Federer's win over Tsonga in the quarters set up another showdown with Djokovic.

Both Federer and Djokovic played well in the first set, with Federer winning in a tiebreak, 9-7. Federer took the second set 6-4 to go up two sets. Djokovic, however, made a run to win the next two sets to even the match.

Federer was able to refocus in the fifth and get up a break. This gave him an opportunity to serve for a berth in the finals. Federer had two match points on his serve. However, the momentum completely changed when Federer hit a wide serve on the deuce court and Djokovic lunged to hit a forehand return for a winner. It was the shot that changed the match. Djokovic ended up tying the set at 5-5 and won the next two games to win the match.

For Federer, he was truly heartbroken and upset. It was one of his toughest defeats. His frustration was obvious after the match. Losses like this are the type to set a player back. But Federer is no ordinary player. He somehow got back up and showed that he could put this loss behind him. The true champion in him emerged and he finished the season incredibly strong.

Federer was back to winning matches. He won again in his hometown in Basel and then Paris. Federer would also go on to win his 6th ATP Finals (which included beating Nadal in the round robin). It would be an impressive finish for 2011 for the 30-year old Federer.

Over the next few years, Federer would experience injury setbacks but would rack up impressive numbers and prove he was still competing with the best. In 2012 he beat Andy Murray to win his 7th Wimbledon title and 17th major overall.

His most difficult year on the tour came in 2013. He was playing an extremely busy schedule that took its toll on Federer and did not leave him enough recovery time. As a result, Federer would have back problems through most of that year- his only title coming in Halle, Germany.

Coming off injury, in 2014 Federer used the opportunity to make a couple of changes to his game. Even the best players know that there is always room for improvement and adapting is essential to remaining competitive. Federer decided to upgrade to a lighter racquet and he also hired legend Stefan Edberg as his coach. In this strategic move, Federer was going to recommit to the serve and volley under Edberg. This would allow him to play shorter points and look for his opportunity to rush the net.

On paper, he was still not achieving the results he once did, but Federer was still among the best and playing high quality tennis. His wins included titles in Halle and Basel as well as Shanghai in 2014 and he appeared in a hard-fought Wimbledon Final against Novak Djokovic once again.

After another major-less season in 2015, questions about whether Roger Federer could win another major. The upside is that it was by all other metrics a successful season. He had a top 3 finish demonstrating his incredible consistency. Federer won 6 titles with one Masters 1000 and a record of 63-11.

A shortened season in 2016 followed as Federer suffered his first major injury in his career. After a semifinal loss in Australia to Novak, Federer went home and banged up his knee while at home giving his kid a bath. It was a freak injury unrelated to the sport. But it was serious enough that Federer would have knee surgery and miss a large portion of the season.

He came back quickly and played three tournaments on the clay, but he probably came back a little too early. As a result, he had to miss the French Open. It would be Federer's first ever major missed due to injury.

Not wanting to miss Wimbledon, Federer came returned

stronger and navigated his way through the tournament with a dramatic quarterfinal win over Marin Cilic. However, he eventually fell to Canadian Milos Raonic in the semifinals. A few weeks later Federer made an announcement that he was not going to play the rest of the year in order to rest his knee.

There was no question that Roger Federer was missed on the tour. The retirement question came from the fans and media. But Federer had other plans. He went to work and hired Ivan Ljubicic as his coach in 2016. The two worked together on figuring out ways to adjust Federer's game. Federer was committed to playing with a lighter racquet, and Ljubicic worked on Roger's one-handed backhand to make it a weapon.

One remaining appearance Roger Federer made that year was to Rafael Nadal's new tennis academy. Unfortunately, both Federer and Nadal were too injured to play an exhibition, but Federer was there to support his rival and friend, someone for whom he had great respect.

The next year, prior to the 2017 Australian Open, Federer played some tune-ups. He admitted he was not among the favorites in Australia and was going to play his way in the tournament hoping to get as far as the fourth round. He did not expect more than that. The favorites were Djokovic and Murray. Djokovic had won 5 of the last 6 Australian Opens, and Murray was #1 in the world.

Federer entered Australia as the 17th seeded player. He would have a very tough draw. He was a 35-year old player who could be playing on the senior tour. In the first round he was up against veteran Jurgen Melzer of Austria. Melzer was a tricky lefty player who could upset the big guns on a given day. Federer would defeat Melzer in four sets. Federer won his second-round match without incident and was about to face a tough test in the third round against Berdych. Prior to the match, Federer stated this would be a good measuring stick to see where his game was. Federer easily dispatched Berdych in three sets.

Federer's movement on the court was phenomenal as were his serve and return.

Up next was 5th seed Ken Nishikori who was playing well. Federer lost the first set in a tiebreak, but got the second and third sets to take a two sets to one lead. Nishikori fought back to even the match. With plenty of fuel in the tank, Federer won the fifth set and advanced to the quarters.

The quarterfinals were expected to be a showdown between Murray and Federer. However, Murray was upset by the veteran Mischa Zverev. Federer would have little trouble getting by Zverev to advance to the semifinals.

Even Federer could not have imagined advancing this far in his first big tournament back. Friend and fellow rival Stan Wawrinka would be the opponent. Wawrinka would be coming off winning the U.S. Open. Wawrinka had won three consecutive majors in the last three years and actually was now the #1 Swiss player. Federer would get out of the gates fast winning the first two sets. Wawrinka fought back to win the next two sets. Federer would break and take the fifth set 6-3 to gain a berth into the finals.

Nadal was awaiting Federer in the finals. The whole tennis world embraced this matchup. Even the players themselves would admit it was a big deal, a very special final. It was more than just another Championship match, it would be two living legends playing once more for a title, when both were written off. To nearly everyone's surprise Federer and Nadal were both back playing at a high level.

The showdown did not disappoint. Federer used his new-found backhand as a weapon that threw a wrench in Nadal's strategy. Nadal came into the match expecting to serve in the ad court to Federer's backhand as well as rip a forehand in that direction to expose his opponent's weakness. This Federer was able to defend against this strategy and was playing offense from this position, giving as good as he got. After several hours of intense tennis, down a break in the fifth set 3-1, Federer won the next five games to win his 18th major. It was his first major title in almost 5 years. The match was a defining moment in an already storied career. The fact that it was against his fiercest rival and that Federer dug deep to win out the fifth set was even sweeter for him. After the match, Roger had a special moment with his wife Mirka and his team. Roger was back.

The Fed wave continued to the sunshine double. Federer would face Nadal early at Indian Wells and easily beat him 6-2, 6-3. Federer was completely in the zone. He faced Stan Wawrinka in the finals. Wawrinka gave Federer a fight, but Federer was too much for him and won 6-4, 7-5. It was Federer's first title at Indian Wells in 5 years.

Surprisingly, Federer decided to play in Miami, when everyone thought he would sit it out to rest. Federer would once again defeat Nadal in the finals to take the Miami title and the sunshine double for the first time in 11 years. Federer at 35 was playing like he was 25. It was clearly his best tennis in 8 years.

Knowing he was 35 and coming off an injury, Federer skipped the clay court season to rest, spend it with his family, and get ready for Wimbledon. The downside was that it would give Federer little chance to get back the #1 ranking. Yet, it was not even on Federer's radar to reach the peak ranking. Winning another Wimbledon was the priority.

Federer played his finest tennis at the 2017 Wimbledon championships. He did not lose a set, and never went down a break n any set. It was a dominant display by the veteran winning his 8th Wimbledon title passing Sampras. It would also be Roger's 19th overall major distancing himself from Nadal who happened to capture his 15th major at Roland Garros a month earlier.

Before the Us. Open though, Federer injured his back once again in the finals at Montreal. He was playing well throughout the tournament but chose to skip Cincinnati to rest and be ready for the U.S. Open.

Federer was very happy to be back in New York after missing it the previous year. Even though Federer stated he was fine his game was off and appeared uncomfortable throughout the fortnight. Federer would lose to Del Potro in the quarters. Nadal was the eventual Champion that year.

Prior to heading into the home stretch in 2017, the inaugural Laver Cup was played, where Team Europe faced Team World. There was some great tennis and fans got a treat with Federer and Nadal playing doubles together for the first time ever.

As the ATP Finals approached, Federer's back was healed, and he looked sharp at Shanghai avenging his U.S. Open loss to Del Potro in the semifinals. Federer would then defeat Nadal in the finals 6-4, 6-3 and win all four matches they played in 2017.

Federer would also win in Basel and appeared a lock to win his 7th ATP Finals Championship. After going undefeated in his round robin, Federer was upset in the semifinals by frequent hitting partner David Goffin of Belgium.

It would be an end to an amazing comeback season. Federer played some of his finest tennis as he turned 36. He finished with the #2 ranking and was 4-0 against the #1 ranked Nadal. Federer won 52 matches and lost 5. He won two majors and three Masters 1000 titles and 7 titles overall.

At the 2018 Australian open the 36-year old Federer won his 6th Australian Open title and became the first male tennis player to win 20 majors. A few weeks later, Federer would return to be the #1 player in the world.

One thing is certain, and that is that Roger Federer's consistency through the years is unmatched. Once able to align his mind to his talent and catch up with his variety, the sky was the limit.

In 20 years on the tour, Federer has won 20 major titles. He has been #1 for five years, and he only finished below the #3 ranking twice between 2003 and 2017. From 2005 to 2007, he appeared in 10 consecutive major finals, winning 8 of them. When that streak was snapped, he appeared in another 8 consecutive major finals, winning 4 of them. Federer also appeared in 23 consecutive major semifinals between 2004 and 2010. He also appeared in 36 consecutive quarterfinals between 2004 and 2013, another record. These records will likely hold for many years to come.

WHAT WE CAN LEARN FROM ROGER FEDERER

Authenticity

R oger Federer exhibits authenticity on and off the court. It is why fans and the media are drawn to him. It is un-surprising that he has won the fan favorite award since 2003. On the court he plays the game with grace and beauty. He is among the greatest tennis players ever to play the game. But for how untouchable he has been at times on the court, his boy-ish laugh and humble demeanor remind us that he is human.

Federer remains extremely down to earth. He is playful and joy-ous during interviews and press conferences and gives his time to his fans, especially the kids. He is well-known to be very intelligent, honest, open and articulate. He knows how much he means to the game and the people. He is classy no matter whether he wins or loses.

Balance:

With all that he has been able to achieve, Roger Federer is a great example of balance in his life. He is not also an iconic tennis player, his is also a great family man. He and his wife, Mirka, have an incredible relationship, and Federer is a very supportive and active father to his four kids. His incredible life balance and achievements characterize an extraordinary quality of life. We can all aspire to achieving our own version of an extraordinary life, just like Roger Federer.

World-renowned life coach and motivational speaker Tony Robbins teaches that an extraordinary quality of life comes down to mastering two skills: "The Science of Achievement" and "The Art of Fulfillment." We don't know for certain whether Roger Federer learned of these skills through Tony Robinson, but his has implemented them. Federer has mastered both areas. Even if Federer had not become a superstar tennis player or a multi-millionaire, he would still have an extraordinary quality of life by any measure.

Achievement & Fulfillment:

In Tony Robbins' best selling book, "Unshakeable," he explains the science of achievement is that in every field there are "rules to success" that we can break or follow. If we break the rules, we will fail or even perhaps suffer. For every rule we follow, we can have success and achievement. Federer follows the rules on what it takes to be a top tennis player. He has achieved every-thing imaginable in tennis by training his mind and body to prepare for every season and match in order to stay consistently at the top of the game. Federer found out in his late teens that talent alone was not going to elevate him to the top of the game. He followed the rules to be a successful player and has been able to win 20 major titles.

Each of us can look at what we want to achieve and then figure out what the rules are to get the result we want. For example, if optimal health is what you want, you may research to learn you need proper rest, physical activity, and a sensible diet to have a healthy mind and body- one that is consistently energized. And you might learn that if you do not follow the rules and eat poorly, you will feel like less-than-optimal and perhaps even get sick.

The same principles apply for wealth or any other thing you desire. If you model wealthy individuals and their investment and money management strategies, you will likely have that success. No matter what our backgrounds are, we can all be wealthy if we follow the rules.

Success leaves clues, and Roger has left us clues to follow his path. Not that we are going to win Wimbledon, but we can achieve our own success in our own field. We can be the Roger Federer of Engineers, Accountants, Nurses, or a firefighter.

The second skill that we all seen Roger master in his life is the art of fulfillment. Unlike the science of achievement where there are rules to follow, the art of fulfillment is different for everyone. One like me loves tennis and someone else might think tennis is incredibly boring where it is just hitting the ball back and forth.

The art of fulfillment is mastering our internal world by growing and giving. Roger is completely fulfilled. Roger is growing as a person constantly seeking to be a better person on and off the court. As we can see in many interviews and public appearances, Roger is very comfortable and at peace on who he is as a person.

The 2nd principle on the art of fulfillment is that we have to give, and Roger is one of the biggest givers and contributors we have seen. The Roger Federer Foundation has nearly served one million children. Roger has spent time in Africa with many of these children as well. Roger's main focus is working to improve the quality of education in South Africa.

If we don't step up and give, there is only so much we can feel inside. We don't have to give massive amounts like Roger. We can donate as little as $5 or $10 or spend an hour at a rest home or shelter. You will find it incredibly fulfilling to give back. As we can see with Roger, giving back is such a mission for him. What fame has done for Roger is just make him more of a giver.

Constantly Improving:

Another way we can model Roger and his consistency is to never stay constant and never be complacent. Always strive to improve and constantly grown in your field and as a person. Roger states that he actually appreciates losing a match. Losing matches gives Roger the opportunity to ponder and look at his game.

At age 36, Roger is still winning majors and actually became # 1 in the world. We accomplish feats like Roger by always constantly and never end in improving ourselves. Roger's one weakness was he did not have a powerful backhand shot. Roger was able to develop that shot into a weapon and won the 2017 Australian Open.

Like Roger, we need to always look at areas we need to improve upon. For Warren Buffet, he struggled with presentation. Thus, he modeled successful speakers as well as enrolled in a Dale Carnegie speaking class. The one certificate Warren Buffet has in his office is Carnegie's class certification. To Mr. Buffet, public speaking is an invaluable skill to have.

We also need to keep improving our strengths no matter what they are. Robert DeNiro is constantly working on his acting skills and trying to get better all the time in order to continually and consistently make critically acclaimed movies. It is also the same with Roger during his dominant years. As Roger stated once, he is constantly looking for ways to improve his overall game and movement on the court, in which he will not become predictable to his opponents.

The reality is that we never stay constant. We are either moving up or moving down. If Roger doesn't always look to improve every aspect of his game and other areas of his life, he and his skills will decline.

The benefits of improving are that it creates positive momentum in your business and personal life. It will be more difficult for your competitors to catch up. Improving creates fulfillment because we are consistently growing, and it is key that we look to improve in all areas of life, not just our business or trade.

Calmness and Sportsmanship:

Another thing we can learn from Roger is calmness, maturity, and sportsmanship. The ATP awards the Stefan Edberg Sportsmanship Award, and Roger has won the award 13 times.

One of Roger's biggest turnarounds is when he started to stay calm and not panic on the court. Prior to 2003, Roger was mentally all over the place. He was losing his cool by smashing racquets and losing his concentration. Roger also could not put his talented game together not knowing what shot to hit at a crucial moment and became stressful.

Since Roger became a champion, Roger has always remained composed in crucial situations, even when he does not win all the time. As Roger says, "Every time I am under pressure, I think of the hard work I have done to get where I am now". Roger trusts the process because he know that he has done the preparation. We need to trust the process ourselves whether we are giving a presentation or working on that particular project because we are prepared.

Also being calm under pressure develops a positive mindset and psychology. Roger is very positive on and off the court. Success is 80% psychology and 20% mechanics. Once Roger changed his psychology, everything came together and became one of the greatest tennis players of all time.

What we have to do before learning anything whether starting your own business, making that presentation, or even starting a relationship is to develop a strong mindset. When things get tough and they will, your psychology and ability to stay calm will pull you through the most difficult of circumstances. Another great example is the 2017 Australian Open Final. When Roger goes down a break in the 5th set against Nadal, Nadal practically owned Federer and had him on the ropes again. Roger remained calm and trusted the process and went on to win the last 5 games of the 5th set after being down 3-1. As a result, Roger won the match and won his 18th major title.

Thus, we need to remain composed and develop our psychology to get the results we desire to have in life. Ways to develop our psychology is to develop rituals that will enable us to get into a positive state. We can do this by asking ourselves empowering questions and create incantations which are affirmations by using our voice and body along with the words.

Set Short Term and Long Term Goals:

What we can also learn from Roger and be consistent is to create short term and long term goals. When Roger got to number one, he decided to make a decision. He decided that he wanted to play tennis at a high level into his 30's. The best method Roger did that was to balance his schedule each year efficiently. Roger's schedule would enable to play the most significant and desired tournaments, but not play too many tournaments.

Roger in his mid 20's knew he had to play the tournaments that had the highest points like majors and the masters 1000s, so he can remain #1 in the world. In his 30's when #1 was no longer his priority, Roger cut back on tournaments and increased his workload in practice and remaining fit. The last few years, Roger has actually missed the entire clay court season which consists of two months of tennis. Roger's focus is to win majors in his 30's and peak at the right time.

Setting short term and long term goals are vital to having any form of success. The famous study of the Yale University class of 1953 provides evidence of how valuable and significant goal setting is. Twenty years after the class of 1953 graduated researchers tracked down the same cohort and found that 3% of people who had specific goals accumulated more personal wealth than the other 97% of their classmates combined.

The benefits of having short term goals are it gives you momentum by creating wins and milestones. For example becoming a doctor would be a long term goal if one is 18 and getting out of high school. Short term goals would be chunked together in this long term goal, such as completing 1st year of college, getting a Bachelor's Degree, and getting into medical school. These short-term goals will keep you motivated for the long term goal(s) and gives you consistently just like Roger has on the tennis court for many years now.

Roger's goal for winning Wimbledon and being #1 were achieved. It was achieved by setting short term goals along the way like turning pro and winning his first pro tournament.

No question goal setting is the recipe for sustaining consistency and success. Goal setting also gives us a compelling future and provides a sense of purpose in life.

With goal setting in Roger's repertoire, he is committed to his outcome. Yet Roger is also flexible in his approach. Roger's flexibility has been demonstrated by changing his game from getting new voices on his team like Stefan Edberg in 2014. Stefan got Roger to serve and volley more and shorten the points. In 2016, Ivan Ljubicic took over and worked with Roger on hitting a more powerful and precise one-handed backhand. Lastly, Roger finally gave into changing tennis racquets. Switching to a lighter racquets, gave Roger less stress on his motion and more power on his shots.

Flexibility creates choice too. We can get to our ultimate goal much quicker as well. Sometimes it be updating a software or system that gets our project complete or makes our day to day job more efficient. Also finding new study method could get one to pass the bar exam much quicker as opposed to the previous approach.

Having the flexibility will open us to new and incredible opportunities that will enhance and improve the quality of our lives in many ways.

Beliefs – The Birth to Excellence:

Belief is something we can learn from Roger as well. Some call it "fake it until you make it". Roger realized that in order to become a champion, he had to first begin thinking like one. This made a massive difference to his career. Unfortunately, most players and people in life think the opposite. Players believe that once they start winning matches, the belief will come. Roger, however; discovered that it is the other way around. The secret is to first create the belief before you begin winning lots of matches.

We can create these beliefs as well. One is to create a compelling vision. We need to create a vision on what we want to accomplish and act like we have accomplished it already. For Roger, it was to act like a champion. Roger saw himself holding that Wimbledon trophy many times before he did win it.

Lastly, we need to make sure we continue to have motivating factors. For Roger, his biggest moment came after losing the first round at the French Open in 2003. Roger asked himself, "was I always going to be the talent that did not have the big result?". Once month later, Roger silenced his critics winning Wimbledon and his first major. Pete Sampras had a similar situation losing the 1992 U.S. Open to Stefan Edberg after realizing he did not have the hunger to win the open. The loss drove Sampras to become the best player in the world.

We all need to find that why and the motivating factor that not only gets us to our ultimate goal, but also get us to live each and every day with purpose and passion.

For Roger Federer, he has become perhaps tennis' greatest champion winning a record 20 major titles. Roger has given us a platform and many clues how to live our lives and succeed. Roger is an artist on the court. Yet, he also has rituals and strategies that we can all learn from and apply into our lives to be the Roger Federer in our own life.

2017 AUSTRALIAN OPEN FINAL

Being the only player in ATP history to win 20 major singles titles, Roger Federer has an entire library of epic matches which could be featured here. Some include non-final matches like his breakthrough 2001 Wimbledon 4th round match with Pete Sampras, or the 2004 U.S. Open quarterfinals against Andre Agassi. Among the legendary major finals that he has been a part of, it would be easy to include his first ever title at Wimbledon in 2003 or his first and only French Open title in 2009.

The match that ultimately displays Roger's consistency may be the 2017 Australian Open Final win. Although he has been known for dominating Wimbledon, this match was chosen because of his performance in the face of numerous challenges. At the time, it was questionable whether Federer would again regain his consistent form in 2017 after his longest layoff from injury. For the first time in 14 years, Federer was not among the favorites heading into the tournament. He was expectations were limited to reaching the third round and getting in some match play. The consensus among experts was that Federer would slowly play his way into the season and be back in form by Wimbledon.

Road to the Final:

Going into 2017, it had been almost five years since Federer had last won a major. He would play well in his first two matches defeating veteran Jurgen Melzer in four sets and American Noah Rubin in three. The first significant test of was to come against Thomas Berdych in the third round. Going up against a top 10 player would show everyone where Federer was in his comeback. Both players knew each other's games well, and Berdych had previously had success against Federer.

Federer beat Berdych without much difficulty. It helped that he played aggressively against Berdych from the get-go. One thing that did stand out was Roger Federer's new-and-improved backhand. Throughout his career the backhand seemed to be the single blemish in Federer's game. However, in his return, he was hitting the backhand early and with authority. I appeared that the six months of long practices and working with Ivan Ljubicic was paying dividends in match play.

In his fourth-round match, Federer faced 5th ranked Kei Nishikori. It was well-played by both, with Federer prevailing in five sets. In the quarters, he faced Mischa Zverev (who had upset Andy Murray in the previous round). Federer took the match in three sets to gain an unlikely semi-finals berth.

As Fed fans were crossing their fingers to get to the finals, something interesting was happening on the other side of the men's draw. Two-time defending champion Novak Djokovic was out in the 2nd round. At the same time, another comeback story began to materialize. Rafael Nadal was coming off a long layoff with a wrist injury. He had struggled massively during the last two years but in this tournament, he sent the message that he was back. Like Federer, Nadal was once again playing at a high level.

Nadal would face Grigor Dimitrov in the semis, and Federer would face friend and rival Stan Wawrinka. Both semifinals would reach five sets. Nadal defeated a gritty Dimitrov. Meanwhile, Federer let a two sets to love lead slip through his hands and allowed Wawrinka to get back in the match. Yet Federer took the fifth set and was on the way to the finals.

A Dream Final:

Australia would get the final that tennis fans dreamed of but never expected- a matchup between Roger Federer and Rafael Nadal. Celebrities from around the world were demanding tickets and flying into Melbourne. The pre-match hype was well-deserved.

Prior to this tournament, it had appeared that reigns of men's tennis had belonged to Djokovic and Murray. Everyone was surprised to see the re-emergence of the Federer-Nadal rivalry. With the Williams sisters playing in the women's finals and Federer and Nadal playing in the men's side, it was a celebration for tennis.

For Roger Federer, it would mean facing his biggest and most difficult rival. At this point, Federer Roger was the underdog to Nadal. Despite winning their last meeting in 2015, Federer was 11 (wins) and 23 (losses) against Nadal. He had also lost all three Australian Open matches he had played against the Spaniard, including the 2009 finals.

The First Set:

Nadal served the first game and held at love. Federer returns the favor and holds his serve to even the set score at 1-1. Both players are moving well and getting a feel for the other. On the opening point of the third game Federer hits a magnificent 93 mph forehand winner down the line. Despite this, Nadal holds to put the set score at 2-1 on serve. Federer then played a brilliant game on his serve, he was aggressive and hit a couple of winners, 2-2. Nadal then held at love to bring the set score to 3-2 on serve. Federer would also hold at love to make it 3-3.

With the match even at three games apiece and Nadal serving, Federer was aggressive on the return to make it 0-15. A few points later, Federer played another great point to make it 15-40 and earn a breakpoint. On the next point, Nadal's wide forehand gave Federer the break, 4-3. At this point in the match there is no sign of the old Federer who had struggled massively in many of his matchups with Nadal. Federer easily holds to for a set score of 5-3.

At 3-5, Nadal finally hits his first forehand winner and holds. However, Federer has an opportunity to serve for the set. After losing the first point, Federer wins the next four points to take the first set, 6-4. Roger Federer looked sharp, especially on the serve.

The Second Set:

With Nadal serving first, he was looking to get off to a fast start and send a message to Federer. He managed to hold and then break Federer on the second game to go up 2-0. Nadal's usual forehand spin was putting Federer into the backhand corner. Federer was unphased by this strategy and gained another breakpoint chance. However, Nadal was able to hold for a set score of 3-0.

On the back of several strong service games, Nadal was able to win the second sent at a score of 6-3.

The Third Set:

Going into the third set, it was anyone's match. We saw Federer draw first blood in the first set showing some tremendous poise and brilliant shot making. As expected, Nadal charged out the gates in the second set, went up two breaks, and managed to take the set. Federer, however, did not hit the panic button. He got back in the match and remained competitive with Nadal.

With Federer serving to start the third set, Nadal hit his beautiful forehand down the line for a winner at 40 love and scraped his way back to deuce. Nadal would then earn a breakpoint.

Federer served an ace to bring the score back to deuce. Nadal would have Federer on the ropes a couple more times, but Federer escaped to hold on serve at 1-0 in the third set.

With Nadal serving the next game at 0-15, Federer hit a beautiful cross court winner for a score of 0-30. Federer stuck to the game plan of hitting the ball tremendously early and staying on the baseline. He was able to hit the backhand down the line and set up his forehand for a breakpoint. Federer capitalized on a Nadal second serve to break and take a lead of 2-0.

A volley winner at 15-0 displayed Federer's willingness to mix it up and keeping Nadal off-balance, 3-0 Federer. With Nadal serving, a brilliant cross-court backhand winner from Federer put him on his heels. Federer was moving brilliantly and getting in the zone. For Nadal, he hoped he could ride out the Federer storm. Nadal managed to get back to deuce. However, Federer hit another great forehand cross-court winner. Nadal served an ace to bring the score back to deuce again. After it appeared that Nadal would escape the game, Federer hit a brilliant backhand return winner. Nadal kept fighting, hitting a forehand winner after a great exchange. Nadal managed to get the next point to hold and make it 3-1. However, Roger was pressuring Nadal unlike ever before.

At 3-1, Federer continued to serve well and held at love to make it 4-1. In the next game, with Nadal serving at 30-30, Federer earns another breakpoint and converts on another backhand return winner to make it 5-1. Again, Federer's backhand is coming up huge and completely dismantling Nadal's game plan.

With Federer serving for the set, Nadal gets a breakpoint. Federer work his way back into the game and makes it deuce on an inside-out forehand winner. Federer earns a set point but shanks a backhand into the net. Federer then hits another unforced error to give Nadal another break, but a great serve makes it deuce. On set point # 2, Federer hits a nice backhand volley winner to take the set 6-1.

The Fourth Set:

With a convincing third set win, Federer seemed to take command of the match. As always though, Nadal was not to be underestimated. There was no way that Nadal was mentally out of this match and Federer knew that. Nadal had come back too many times before.

Nadal served to open the fourth set. Federer hit a backhand return winner at 15-0. Nadal had to have been shell-shocked by Federer's consistency on his backhand. At 30-30, Nadal hit a strong forehand to jam Federer and go up 40-30 and then win the first game.

With Federer to serve, he held to make it 1-1. Nadal then followed up with a routine hold to make it 2-1, on serve. In the next game Federer played two very loose points to go down 0-30. Nadal then earned a triple breakpoint on a forehand winner. Nadal capped the break to go up 3-1.

It is the toughness of Nadal that provides constant pressure. Federer knows he will need to break Nadal back if he is to win this in four sets. Federer's confidence did not waver though and he was still aggressive getting to deuce on Nadal's serve. It took a brilliant defensive cross-court forehand by Nadal to escape and go up 4-1. It appeared Federer had the point with the angle on a brilliant backhand. Yet, Nadal responded beautifully.

At 1-4 and serving, Federer knew he needed to hold to stay in the set. Federer did hold after Nadal did get a breakpoint, 4-2 Nadal. Nadal held at love to make it 5-2. Federer would serve to stay in the match. He struggled on his serve but held to make it 5-3 for Nadal. Nadal would serve for the fourth set and hold easily to win 6-3.

The Fifth Set:

For the fourth time, Rafael Nadal and Roger Federer would play a fifth set major final. The last time was the Australian Open in 2009, where Federer did not play well at all in the 5th set and lost the match.

Federer took an injury timeout before the fifth set, like he did in the semifinals against Stan Wawrinka. Federer would serve first and hope to get off to a fast start. Yet, the momentum of the fourth set carried into the first game. Nadal was locked in and playing at his highest level so far. He earned two breakpoints. After a loose forehand error by Federer, Nadal broke his serve to go up 1-0.

Now, Federer would need to break Nadal twice in order to win this. Nadal just needed to hold the rest of the way to win.

With Nadal serving, Federer tried to chip and charge on the first point, but Nadal prevailed. Federer persisted and earned a double breakpoint of his own. Nadal did manage to get it back to deuce. Federer got another breakpoint on a shot that clipped the net. Nadal held with an incredible winner down the line, 2-0 for Nadal.

At 0-2 and a must hold, Federer held at love. It was easily his best service game since before he was broken in the fourth set. Up a break and serving, Nadal got up 30-0. Federer though comes up with a cross-court backhand winner and score shifts to 30-30. Both exchanged points to get it to deuce. Federer got a breakpoint with another backhand winner displaying outstanding footwork. Nadal fights off the breakpoint with a backhand winner of his own. Nadal manages to win the remaining points and holds to make it 3-1. Federer knocked on the door twice trying to break back, but Nadal held on.

Good news for the Federer camp was that he was fresh and playing well, but they wondered if he would have another chance to break. For Nadal, he needed to just hold serve, but was struggling to do so in his two service games.

Federer serving at 1-3 and would hold relatively easy to make it

3-2 in favor of Nadal. With Nadal serving, Federer goes up 0-30, after an unforced error by his opponent. Nadal got a point back to make it 15-30 on an unforced error by Federer. The game score then became 30-30 on a great serve wide by Nadal that Federer just got back to set up an easy winner. Federer though earns a breakpoint to make it 30-40 on a long ball by Nadal. Deuce # 1 was a serve and easy winner from Nadal. Nadal then won the advantage on a Federer return to the net. Nadal commits an unforced error creating Deuce #2. Breakpoint comes for Federer on another backhand winner. With another break point, a brief rally by Federer and Nadal ends when Nadal hits a forehand wide. Federer breaks back to make it 3-3 in the fifth set. Federer showed tremendous will and hustle on that return game. Now it was time for him to serve and hopefully hold and put the pressure back on Nadal.

At 3-3 in the fifth set, the fans are all cheering and giving both players a well-deserved standing ovation. Federer opens up with an ace and then goes up 30-0 with a forehand volley winner. Federer makes it 40-0 on a return error by Nadal. Federer then hits a second serve ace and takes the game. It is 4-3 Federer, and the players are on serve.

Nadal hoped he could get back the momentum at 3-4 on his serve. He had the momentum in the fourth set and start of the fifth set. Nadal had been in this position before and has won. Unfortunately, it did not start well for Nadal as an incredible slice by Federer forced an error, 0-15. It became 0-30 on the back of some brilliant shot making by Federer, who seemed to be on the zone. A double fault gave Federer triple break point.

As always, Nadal refused to quit getting one back to make it 15-40. A long return by Federer makes it 30-40. It becomes Deuce # 1 on a backhand return error by Federer, who now appeared a little tight knowing that he was close to the finish line.

At Deuce, and with Nadal on his second serve, the point of the match is played. It was an absolutely incredible 25-shot rally.

Federer looked to be in trouble early however escaped and then appeared to be in control on to get neutralized again. Finally, Federer patiently gets Nadal way over on the backhand side to open the court. As a result, Federer hits a forehand winner down the line.

It is a point that is played time and time again on YouTube and other highlights. It could have been Federer's finest moment at that point. The rally displays the beauty, talent, and brilliance of both players. Federer gets the point and gets another well-earned break opportunity. Naturally the crowd is on its feet.

Nadal gets it back to deuce on an ace. However, Federer finds an opening on his forehand and forces another Nadal error. Federer has his fifth breakpoint of the game and keeps the pressure on Nadal.

This time Federer converts the breakpoint on another great backhand return that Nadal cannot do anything with but swings it wide. All of a sudden, it was 5-3 and Federer was about to serve for the championship. Federer dug incredibly deep coming back from down a break to being up a break.

Going into the service game, Federer and Fed fans knew it was not going to be easy. There was no way Nadal was going to lie down to Federer. That is what happened as Nadal goes up 0-15 on a backhand return cross-court winner on Federer's second serve. Another second serve by ends in an unforced error and gives Nadal a 0-30 lead in the game. Federer calms his nerves with an ace to make it 15-30.

Nadal earns a double break point with an easy put away at the net, 15-40. Suddenly, the match could get back to on serve and keep going. There is no 5th set tiebreaker as well.

Federer gets one back with his second ace of the game, 30-40. On the next point Nadal has a second serve opportunity but Federer hits a beautiful inside-out forehand to make it deuce. A long forehand by Nadal gives Federer a championship point.

To add to the drama of the moment, it appears Federer double faulted, but after challenging the call it is determined he had not. It is a first serve, but Federer hit it wide. A second serve by Federer was returned by Nadal and forced a long forehand by Federer which brought he game score back to deuce.

At deuce, Federer hit his third ace to earn another championship point.

Federer's next serve set him up for a potential winner and he converts it by hitting the line on Nadal's backhand side. Since Nadal has a challenge, he takes a chance to see if the shot possibly had gone wide. But the shot is called "in", and Federer has won the 2017 Australian Open. It becomes his first major win in almost five years. Federer also beats Nadal for the first time in a major in almost ten years. The way Federer does it by coming back in the fifth makes it all that more special.

At age 35, Roger has just won his biggest match ever. It is his 18th major title and an unbelievable and near improbable comeback. It was a great comeback in the fifth set again the biggest clutch tennis player. As Patrick McEnroe states, "Roger out-Rafa-ed Rafa". Federer showed more guts and desire than he ever did before in his illustrious career.

Federer won the 2017 Australian Open with a score of 6-4, 3-6, 6-1, 3-6, 6-3. The score indicates the fifth set was one-0sided, but it clearly was not. Both players played at an incredibly high level. Nadal played great, but Federer was brilliant and a little better.

Six months ago, Federer and Nadal had been written off and were no longer considered at the top of their game. The Australian Open final proved, once again, their staying power. It was an exciting matchup that lived up for the hype. The real winner on this night was tennis, and it was the biggest night for the great Roger Federer.

CONTRIBUTION AND THE WILLING TO GIVE
THE BIG FOUR

WHAT WE CAN LEARN FROM MURRAY, DJOKOVIC, NADAL, AND FEDERER

The Power of Service

Although there are countless lessons that we can learn from these four incredible champions, one very strong feature they each share is a love of service and contribution. Federer, Nadal, Djokovic, and Murray have all used their abilities to serve and give back to others and their communities. Tony Robbins says, "the secret to living is giving," and "only those who have learned the power of sincere and selfless contribution experience life's deepest joy; true fulfillment." The ability to give and contribute transforms your life and others. We all have the ability to touch other people's lives and giving, along with the practice of gratitude, will give you a life of fulfillment.

We can all be like one of these great champions serving one another and our communities. It does not take large sums of money nor an extraordinary amount of time to give back to others. Do not wait to achieve your life goals to become a contributor. Do it now. Do it in small amounts. Once you give to others, you will feel abundant and feel there is more than enough to give. An abundant mindset makes us wealthy and allows us to give.

There are many organizations that you can join and contribute to and if you're looking for a place to start, the big four have their own organizations they support that you can learn about.

Roger Federer has established he Roger Federer Foundation whose main focus is to provide educational support in South Africa. Rafael Nadal also has his own foundation, The Rafael Nadal Foundation. Its main goal is to help socially disadvantaged children who run the risk of exclusion by society. The Novak Djokovic Foundation provides every child the opportunity to receive a quality preschool education. Andy Murray supports many charities in his community associated with disaster relief, human rights, and hunger. He also serves as the UNICEF UK Ambassador. UNICEF is one of the largest charitable organizations in the world and a partner of the ATP (Association of Tennis Professionals). It provides education, vaccines, and emergency relief for children among its many other functions.

Listed below are the respective websites for the Big Four. If you want to research more and perhaps serve in any of them:

The Roger Federer Foundation www.rogerfedererfoundation.or/en/home	Novak Djokovic Foundation www.novakdjokovicfoundation.org
The Rafael Nadal Foundation www.fundacionrafanadal.org/en	Andy Murray - UNICEF UK www.unicef.or.uk/celebrity-supporters/andy-murray/

THANK YOU FOR YOUR LOVE AND SUPPORT – ACKNOWLEDGMENTS

ACKNOWLEDGMENTS

As with any project or anything in life, this book definitely does not get down alone. It is only right to thank those that helped me out with this book and got me to this point in my life.

My first shout out needs to go to my partner and editor in this project, Laura Santiago. Thank you for your hard work and sharing the love of tennis with me.

I also need to thank my life partner and loving wife, Carmen. I love you my dear. I also want to thank the person who introduced me to the game of tennis many years ago, my father. In addition, I want to thank my mother as well as my siblings: Laura, Cynthia, and Donald. Lastly thank you to my nieces and nephew Caroline, Lauren, Anna and Max.

I also want to thank my tennis and coffee buddy, Sanja. Thank you Sanja for your feedback on this project. I can't wait to see you at the Miami Open and future tennis tournaments. I also want to thank my other tennis friend, Doug. Doug and I were track teammates in High School and have been friends ever since. I would also like to thank the instructors and peers at the Weymouth Tennis Club. It is fun to get to play this great game.

In addition, I want to thank Vivaldi and Maya for their love and friendship through the years. Also, my fellow Boston sports friends, Al and Stevo, thank you for everything. I also am thankful for those friends and teammates that I have had for the longest time. There are many to mention and all of you mean the world to me.

I want to thank my mastermind group who encouraged me to do this project and were there for me: Cindy, John, Andrew, and Ryan. Thank you Cindy for advising me to make sure that this book combines self development and tennis which are two incredible passions of mine.

To all the coaches and mentors in my life. Stefan of Project Life Mastery, thank you for coaching me. Also, thank you for introducing me to the online business. Coach Prev, thank you for your wisdom and advice. You are the greatest teacher I have ever had.

I also want to thank some who I never met: Tony Robbins, Wayne Dyer, Oprah, and Marianne Williamson. These are the Big Four for me when it comes to self development. I actually did get to meet Tony many years ago. I was introduced to self development many years ago when Tony would show up on those late night infomercials.

Lastly, I want to thank Roger Federer, Rafael Nadal, Novak Djokovic, and Andy Murray for this book is about. Thank you for giving us the greatest era in men's tennis.

ABOUT MISSION FULFILLMENT

J amie Sierra shares his journey to his mission to living life with fulfillment by making progress and improvement in every area in life whether it is your relationships, emotions, spiritual, health, career, finances, or friends and family. Jamie also shares how to create a plan for your life, create and have a strong mindset, as well as identify your beliefs in eliminating limiting beliefs and creating empowering beliefs to take your life to the next level. This channel is dedicated to help you become more confident by living your truth and loving yourself as you continue to discover more of who you are. In addition this channel is designed to help you make progress in every area of your, so you will have joy and happiness. TOPICS: Personal Development, Self Improvement, Spirituality, Health and Wellness, Relationships, Emotional Mastery & Career.

Mission Fulfillment is designed to be a source of self-development, inspiration, and change for those who refuse to settle for anything less than an extraordinary life.

To get started, go to www.missionfulfillment.com

[1] In Andy Murray's autobiography "Seventy-Seven": "When Andy hired Lendl, he felt like he was a loser: nothing more nothing less. 'You wouldn't believe the abuse I would get walking down the street: people would swear and shout at me. If I went on Twitter, there was ridiculous amount of abuse. I felt like a failure, even though I was one of the best in the world. I had won several tournaments; I should have been proud of what I achieved.'

[2] From Murray's autobiography 'Seventy-Seven': "Andy had never been as emotional from a loss as he was from the 2012 Wimbledon. He had been upset losing to Federer in the finals. Yet, Andy was satisfied that he did his absolute best and just had enough. 'Ivan told me that as well as being proud of how I played at Wimbledon, he was impressed by how I'd handle everything that surrounded the tournament'"

[3] That Real Estate Broker was Jennifer Allen and she is now a published author and founded a company called Sell with Soul.

Made in the USA
Middletown, DE
03 August 2019